Meaningful Life Skills

Reproducible Activity Handouts for Older Adults

- Anger and Forgiveness
- Anxiety and Stress
- Coping
- Daily Routine
- Emotional Expression
- Grief / Loss
- Medications
- Mental Illness and Aging
- Reminiscences
- Safety
- Self-Esteem and Self-Awareness
- Social Skills and Leisure
- Spirituality
- Staying Active or Independent
- Thinking Skills

by Estelle A. Leutenberg
and Kathy L. Khalsa, OTR/L

illustrated by
Amy L. Brodsky, LISW

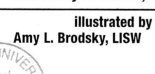

Meaningful Life Skills

Reproducible Activity Handouts for Older Adults

Library of Congress Card Number: 2002117124
ISBN 10: 1-893277-16-X
ISBN 13: 978-1-893277-16-8

Product # 363838

||WELLNESS
||REPRODUCTIONS
||&PUBLISHING

2 Skyline Drive, Suite 101 • Hawthorne, NY 10532
1.800.669.9208 • www.wellness-resources.com

We dedicate *Meaningful Life Skills*

to our twin grandsons / nephews

Kyle Jacob Brodsky and **Tyler Mitchell Brodsky**

born June 15, 2002

who are at the beginning of their life experiences

and

to the memory of

Meyer Atkin

their great-grandfather

whose memories and influences live on.

**Thanks to the following professionals
for their clinical guidance and inspiration:**

Patrick Arbore, Ed.D.   Vicki L. Schmall, Ph.D.

Erlene Rosowsky, Psy.D.   Kathy Laurenhue, M.A.

Foreword

We have published seven reproducible activity handout books of life skills for adults and three for teens. Over the past few years, our customers have expressed an interest in books for older adults. We have designed this book specifically with the older adult in mind. The topics cover issues of concern to older adults, such as loss and grief, depression, anxiety, memory and life transitions.

Meaningful Life Skills is designed for older adults with a variety of needs and abilities. The pages are highly adaptable, so feel free to add, edit or delete text or graphics to make each activity appropriate for your clients. Customizing an activity will enhance the group experience for everyone.

To enable the facilitator to see the handout while reading information on how to facilitate the activity, the book provides the facilitator's information on the top and the reproducible activity handout at the bottom. For each handout, the accompanying Leader's Guide states the purpose, offers a few possible names for the session, gives background information, outlines how to lead the activity, and suggests two variations. Although these suggestions might work perfectly for your group of older adults, we realize they may not. You can use the handouts as a starting point, from which you can create your own activities.

This is a sampler collection of handouts, which are reproducible, organized logically, designed for specific, well-defined purposes, and activity-based, allowing for client involvement. The graphic representations are intentionally different from handout to handout in typestyle, art and design to increase visual appeal, provide variety, and clarify meaning.

We purposely set the book up in landscape format, using 13 to 14 point size for easy readability. The illustrations are fun, interesting and appealing to the older adult. The spiral binding allows you to reproduce the handouts easily and accurately. We have made the book a bit oversized, so the spiral binding will not show in photocopies.

We hope you and your older adults find these handouts fun, innovative and informative. Our goal? Creative handouts will hopefully generate creative activities and contribute to a greater sense of WELLNESS.

If you find these handouts helpful and are inspired to create some of your own, we'd love to hear from you. Our handouts are often contributed by healthcare professionals or educators who have successfully used the activities in their practice. You'll find a submission form on the last page of this book.

Kathy L. Khalsa and Estelle A. Leutenberg – Wellness Reproductions & Publishing

Submittors' Information

After writing the first two books in the *Life Management Skills* series, professionals contacted us from all over the United States and Canada, telling us they had created handouts that would be fitting for these books. When we were ready to write *Life Management Skills III*, we sent a letter to our customers asking if they would like to submit handouts and they did!

The subsequent *Life Management Skills* are filled with activities from a variety of disciplines and on a variety of topics. We have taken several of these submissions and adapted them for this first book in a series for older adults, *Meaningful Life Skills*. We welcome you to submit your handouts for the next books. See the last page in this book for a submission form.

We thank the following facilitators who sent us their submissions!

Holiday Recipe for Disaster, page 8, submitted by **Rebecca August, LCSW.** Rebecca graduated with her MSW in 1998. She currently works part time doing clinical outpatient counseling with adolescents and adults.

Celebrate You, page 49, *Making Transitions,* page 12 and *Understanding My Anger,* page 5, submitted by **Sandra J. Christensen, BA,** Milwaukee, WI. Sandra is a consultant, specializing in training that helps people to achieve their personal and professional goals by increasing self-understanding and improving the ability to communicate effectively with others. In her leisure time, Sandra enjoys reading, biking, running and exploring the world with her young son.

Steps of Grief, page 30, by **Marta Felber, M.Ed.,** West Fork, AR., adapted from Life Management Skills V. Marta's M.Ed. is in counseling. After her husband died, Marta used her experience of more than 30 years in helping professions to heal herself. She is the author of *Grief Expressed: When a Mate Dies.* Walking and traveling to exotic places are among her favorite leisure activities.

The Social Skills Interview, page 60, submitted by **Kelly Fischer, OTR/L,** Baltimore, MD, and **Kim Corbett, OTR/L.** Kelly is an advanced therapist in an acute psychiatric setting, working with adults on maximizing daily living and psychosocial skills so they can return to the community. Kim practices as a staff therapist in both acute inpatient psychiatry and an outpatient day hospital setting.

The Emotions Balloon, page 25, by **Rick Germann, MA, LCPC, RPRP,** Chicago, IL., adapted from *Life Management Skills VII.* Rick is the coordinator of daily operations for an outpatient psychiatric rehabilitation program. He also teaches undergraduate health and graduate counseling courses. Rick's leisure interests are anything outdoors! He is a field editor for an outdoors magazine and "when I'm not at work, I'm usually fishing (with my wife, of course)."

Quick Picks, page 19, submitted by **Martin B. Golub, CTRS,** Rochester, NY. Marty is a Senior Certified Therapeutic Recreation Specialist in an outpatient mental health program for individuals working on achieving and maintaining wellness (and he uses LMS books all the time!) He enjoys bowling, Buffalo Bills football, crafts, family and friends.

Healing from a Loss, page 31, by **Mary Lou Hamilton, MS, RN,** Wilmington, DE. adapted from *Life Management Skills V.* As a Clinical Nurse Specialist, Mary Lou has worked in educational settings for most of her career. Presently a collegiate nurse educator, she teaches her students how to utilize expressive art techniques and journaling activities with patients in psychiatric acute care units. Her favorite leisure activities include painting with watercolors and acrylics, constructing dolls and making pins.

How Does Your Garden Grow?, page 51 and *Reveal How You Feel,* page 27, submitted by **Kimberly D. Heath,** BA in psychology, MA in Art Therapy, Wellsboro, PA. Kimberly is a clinical coordinator for a partial hospitalization program and an intensive outpatient program. She works with individuals ages 18 and older who have a variety of mental health diagnoses. Her leisure activities include crafting and baking with her 8 year-old daughter.

A Year of Events and Traditions, page 57, submitted by **K. Oscar Larson, OTL, MA, BCG,** Alexandria, VA. Oscar has worked 15 years in acute care mental health settings, with an emphasis on older adults. He has presented workshops at local, national and international conferences. In his spare time he is usually chasing woodchucks out of his organic garden.

Good For Me!, page 50, submitted by **Judith A. Lutz,** Belleville, PA. Judy worked for twelve years as a psychiatric counselor in inpatient, IOP and outpatient settings. She is currently working as an employment counselor assisting people with barriers to employment in finding jobs.

If I Could Write a Book, page 24, by **Mark S. Macko, MEd, BS, AAS,** Sarasota, FL., adapted from *Life Management Skills VII*. Mark, a Licensed Mental Health Counselor in Florida, is a rehabilitation counselor. His M.Ed. is in Psychology in Education and his undergraduate degrees are in Psychology (B.S.) and Graphic Art and Design. In his spare time, Mark enjoys creative writing, 12-string guitar, CDs, and music videos.

Who Am I Culturally?, page 56, submitted by **Elana Markovitz, OTRL,** Forest Hills, NY. Elana works with infants and school-aged children experiencing developmental delays, physical disabilities, and learning disabilities to increase performance in the home and school environment. Areas of concentration include fine and gross motor acquisition and development, as well as the use of assistive technology.

Effects of Emotional Abuse, page 22, submitted by **Esterlee A. Molyneux, MS, SSW,** Logan, UT. Esterlee is the program coordinator at a child abuse prevention agency. She teaches parenting skills in a variety of settings, leads a parents' support group, presents an in-school sexual abuse prevention curriculum and is involved with various community agencies. Esterlee is the proud mother of two beautiful girls!

Emergency Information, page 44, *Kitchen Safety,* page 45, *Morning Routine,* page 18 and *Things to Do Before Going to Bed,* page 48, submitted by **Melissa L. Oliver, MS, OTR/L,** Abingdon, VA and **Vicki L. Addison, COTA,** N. Tazewell, VA. They work at a mental health facility with adults and older adults. Vicki enjoys reading and sewing. Melissa enjoys playing tennis and traveling.

How to Make a Friend, page 59, and *What Makes You Happy,* page 55 submitted by **Linda Prib, ADC,** Painesville, OH. Linda is the activity director for a large healthcare facility and plans activities for the assisted living and Alzheimer's units. She is currently working on a project to provide materials for dementia patients to enrich their spiritual lives.

Developing a System That Works for You, page 35, *Fact Sheet,* page 36 and *Do You Know Your Meds,* page 37, by **Joan Rascati,** New Haven, CT., adapted from *Life Management Skills V.* Although retired, Joan continues to write for mental health-related publications. She spent more than 18 years with a mental health agency in New Haven, CT, where she was involved in social, community and independent group living skills programs.

Activities of Daily Living, page 16, submitted by **Regi Robnett, MS, OTR/L, BCN,** South Portland, ME. Regi is an associate college professor, involved in home care and working on her Ph.D. in gerontology. Her interests include mental health, home safety and neurorehabilitation. Regi's leisure hobbies are doing things with her family and dog, bicycling, photography and gardening.

What You Don't Say Counts Too!, page 62, submitted by **Sue Ellen Rosenblum, MOT, OTR/L,** Tampa FL. Sue Ellen has her masters degree from Nova Southeastern University. She is working in a Florida country school system as a school occupational therapist. Sue Ellen enjoys spending time with friends, family and dog, Casey.

Energy Conservation, page 67, *Mental Toughness,* page 70, *Safety First,* page 47, *Stress Symptoms,* page 10, and *Grief Is Like,* page 32, submitted by **Libby D. Schardt, OTR/L,** Omaha, NE. Libby works as a pediatric occupational therapist in the school system. Her hobbies include painting, reading, writing books and water skiing. She also enjoys traveling and spending time with her husband, Brian.

Sing, Sing a Song, page 41, submitted by **Sylvia T. Schwartzman, RN, MS,** Rochester, NY. Sylvia is a program nurse/group facilitator in a continuing day treatment and partial hospitalization program for seniors with mental illness. She plans, leads, and evaluates a variety of groups including Bibliotherapy, Exercise, Travelogue, Wellness, and Health and Well-being. Sylvia enjoys travel, reading, exercise, yoga and shopping.

My Love Letter to Me, page 63, *This New Year's Resolution,* page 64, and *Weathering Spiritual Seasons,* page 65, submitted by **Rev. Donald Shields, BRE, MTS,** Markham, Ontario, Canada. Donald is the coordinator of spiritual and religious care at a hospital. He is pursuing Doctoral studies and hopes to do his project / dissertation in some area of spirituality. Donald is married with two daughters in University and enjoys the arts, reading and animals.

Stress Relief A-Z, page 9, submitted by **Wanda M. Verne, BS,** Jax, FL. Wanda had 10 years of experience in a private psychiatric hospital as a recreation therapist and for the past 10 years has been a clinical manager of two outpatient psychosocial rehab programs for a community mental health center. Her leisure interests are reading, surfing the net, boating and water skiing, sewing and crafting.

My Anger Temperature, page 4, submitted by **Shelley Young, MSW,** Tuscaloosa, AL. Shelley is director of a partial hospitalization program in a residential treatment facility for adults with serious mental illness. The residential facility is affiliated with a community mental health care system in rural Alabama.

Table of Contents – Handouts Listed Alphabetically

Table of Contents - Handouts Listed by Topic

Anger Management

Leader's Guide

Purpose

To manage anger effectively.

Possible Names of Sessions

- "If I Don't Learn to Manage My Anger, then..."
- "Anger"
- "Sometimes, I See Red!"

Background Information

Anger, in and of itself, is not bad. It can make you feel alive and move you to getting something done. But, it can also, if not handled well, be destructive and unhealthy. It is important to emphasize choices.

Activity

1. Offer a few examples of stories you have heard that made you or someone you know angry.

2. Ask others to share the same.

3. Explain that very rarely do people like the feeling of anger. It is not often talked about and easier to identify on others than it is on ourselves. It is also important to recognize that as we live longer, there might be old sources of anger and new ones as well.

4. Distribute handouts and easy-to-read pens.

5. Give group members ten minutes to complete.

6. Share responses.

7. Create a flipchart with all responses from steps 1 and 4.

8. Complete group by going around the room and completing the sentence:
   "If I don't learn to manage my anger, then

   _____

   _____ ".

Variations

1. Discuss medical problems that might be related to stress, anxiety or anger issues.

2. Lead a guided imagery exercise about anger and forgiveness.

Anger Management

Anger is an emotion. It is a normal human response. When anger gets too intense, when it happens too quickly and often, and when it harms self and others... it is time to look at it. Anger can become destructive. Hostility may result in aggressive behavior. **Review these four steps:**

1. Acknowledge, "I'm angry". This awareness is the first step in anger management. This anger may result as a feeling of being threatened, not having power, control or independence. It may stem from feelings of lacking freedom that 'I don't belong.' Give one example of anger you've experienced in the past week. "I'm angry / I was angry that _____

_____".

2. See these choices that are not OK.
- Acting harmfully or violently towards myself
- Acting harmfully or violently towards others

3. Know that anger not handled properly can result in...
- Aggressive behavior
- Guilty feelings
- Health consequences
- Isolation
- Elder Abuse
- Depression

4. Recognize the healthy choices you have and that you can make. When I am in situations where I find myself getting angry, I can:

- leave the situation.
  "I can leave a situation by _____

  _____".

- use self-talk.
  "Last week I could have said to myself, _____

  _____

  _____".

- talk about it.
  "I could talk about it to _____

  _____

  _____".

Forgiveness...
giving up the anger

Leader's Guide

Purpose

To approach forgiveness as a way to release grudges and resolve past hurts.

Possible Names of Sessions

- "Forgive and Forget?"
- "Steps to Forgiveness"
- "Am I Forgiving?"

Background Information

Forgiveness is an often-overlooked topic by the healthcare system and left to theologians. Unfortunately, forgiveness issues may slip through the cracks and be left unresolved or not discussed. In turn, this may be damaging to a person's well-being.

Activity

1. Discuss that forgiving and forgetting a person is not actually possible. We might forgive but not forget. Raise real-life issues that might be relevant, e.g., Will the mother who forgives the drunk driver who hit her daughter, ever forget?

2. Distribute handouts and easy-to-read pens.

3. Give group members fifteen minutes to complete the handout. Emphasize that not forgiving is an option. Use therapeutic judgment if a participant expresses difficulty in forgiving.

4. Share responses in an attitude of acceptance.

5. Discuss what the next step might be in the healing process for each group member.

Variations

1. Raise thought-provoking questions around the topic of forgiveness:
   a. Is it ever all right NOT to forgive?
   b. What are reasons people do not forgive?
   c. What are the benefits of forgiving?

2. Encourage people to explore early messages about forgiveness: Did you live with forgivers or grudge-bearers growing up? Did you ever know any grudge-bearers who couldn't even remember what they were angry about?

Forgiveness... giving up the anger

Forgiveness may be one of the most difficult tasks we humans do. It may seem impossible to forgive at times or it might not be what we want to do, but it may be a wise choice.

The impact of NOT forgiving might be:

• Anger

• Health issues

• Impaired relationships

• _____

• _____

In general, how do you see yourself as a forgiving or not forgiving person?

Not forgiving 0 _____ 10 _Forgiving_
(Put an "x" on the line above.)

What is one current 'forgiveness issue' you have in your life right now? _____

_____

Where are you on the continuum on this current forgiveness issue in your life?

Not forgiving 0 _____ 10 _Forgiving_
(Put an "x" on the line above.)

People who have forgiven (or reconciled) have reported feeling "not conquered by bitterness" and "not giving the person who hurt them the power." How might you feel if you move more towards the forgiving side? _____

_____

If you had the opportunity to say what you wanted to this person (or persons), what would you say? _____

_____

_____

What steps can you take to see the person or persons who betrayed or hurt you as human beings, rather than 'bad', 'evil' or 'monster-like'?

1. _____

2. _____

3. _____

My Anger History

Leader's Guide

Purpose

To promote anger management.

Possible Names of Sessions

- "Meet Your Anger"
- "I Feel Angry When..."
- "ANGER...it's not new"

Background Information

Older adults may have a lot to be angry about - with years of opportunities and situations for losses, disappointments, and betrayals. They have had many years to hold on to anger. Using prompts, they may be able to identify early lessons learned about anger and personal aspects of anger.

Activity

1. Explain purpose and background of group using information at the left.

2. Ask volunteer from the group to sit in front of everyone. Advise him/her that these will be personal questions about anger.

3. Proceed asking him/her questions from the handout.

4. Thank volunteer for sharing openly about a difficult topic.

5. Distribute handouts and easy-to-read pens.

6. Give group members ten minutes to complete handouts.

7. Divide group into pairs for sharing.

8. Reconvene and ask if anyone had any commonalities with his/her partner. Share responses.

9. Process that early influences about anger might be present in older age and may or may not play a healthy role currently.

Variations

1. Have all group members sit in a circle with a parachute and a small ball in the center. Go around the circle asking what people are angry about. They can give responses one by one when they pop the ball into the air with that last burst of energy with the parachute.

2. Ask group members to complete the sentence, *I feel angry when* _____

_____

_____ .

My Anger History

We don't get angry ONLY as older adults. We experienced anger since we were very young, even as babies and toddlers! (Have you ever seen a baby lose a rattle or pacifier or a toddler have a toy taken out of his or her hands?) Fill in the blanks about your anger history.

I have a history of experiencing anger for _____ years.

I learned about anger as a child. I learned that anger is _____.

When I lost _____ , I became angry and I handled this situation by

_____.

When I was disappointed by _____ , I became angry and I managed this

situation by _____.

I feel anger in my body in my _____.

My relationship with my children/grandchildren is **close** 0 1 2 3 4 5 6 7 8 9 10 **distant.**

My relationship with my siblings is   **close** 0 1 2 3 4 5 6 7 8 9 10 **distant.**

When I feel like I can't go on, I say to myself " _____."

What else can I say about my anger? _____

_____

My Anger TEMPERATURE

Leader's Guide

Submitted by
Shelley Lynn Young, MSW

Purpose

To explore causes of anger and ways to cope with anger.

Possible Names of Sessions

- "What Fuels My Anger?"
- "Anger and My Health"
- "Chill Out!"

Background Information

Everyone gets angry from time to time. It is natural to have these feelings. What is important is the reaction to these feelings and how we cope with anger. It is also important to be able to recognize what triggers anger. Repeated anger reactions are harmful to our bodies; anger raises blood pressure, increases heart rates and affects the immune system.

Activity

1. Introduce topic of anger. Ask group members to raise hands if they have ever been angry.

2. Review Background Information.

3. Introduce idea of our bodies being like a thermometer. Explain that as we become angry, our temperatures rise which could be harmful to our bodies as well as our relationships. Coping skills or calming strategies are needed to cool off.

4. Write scale on board:
   - +0 - No anger/no heat
   - +5 - Minimal anger/warm
   - +10 - Moderate anger/getting hot
   - +15 - Severe anger/on fire

5. Distribute worksheets and markers.

6. Ask group members to listen as situations are read that may or may not result in anger. As each situation is read, group members are to use scale on the board to judge their possible reaction. They are to color in the corresponding number of degrees on the thermometer labeled "Heating UP".

7. Vary situations that might elicit anger. Examples might include: You are left out of a family get-together. You are asked again to take care of the grandchildren for a weekend after you already said you couldn't do it again in the next 6 months. You overhear someone in the grocery store making fun of someone who is old and can't hear well.

8. After reading several situations, ask group members to look at their thermometers to see how hot they are (where they stopped coloring). This temperature is to be labeled on the second thermometer labeled "Cooling OFF".

9. Write new scale on the board:
   - -0 - Does not cool me off
   - -5 - Chilly
   - -10 - Frozen

10. Read a series of coping skills and calming strategies to the group. As each strategy is read, ask group members to use new scale to determine how well this strategy would work. For example, a strategy that really helps would decrease the temperature by 10 degrees and a strategy that doesn't help at all would not decrease the temperature at all. Group members are to begin at the temperature marked from "Heating UP" exercise and color corresponding numbers of degrees down. Examples of coping skills and calming strategies are: Take slow, deep breaths, go for a walk, talk to a friend.

11. After several strategies, ask group members to look at temperature they are at on their thermometer.

Variations

1. Before the group session begins or in a separate meeting, ask group members to write on index cards, real-life situations that are anger provoking. Use these cards for your anger prompts for that group.

2. Before the group session begins or in a separate meeting, ask group members to write on index cards, calming strategies or coping skills. Use these cards as prompts in the group.

My Anger TEMPERATURE

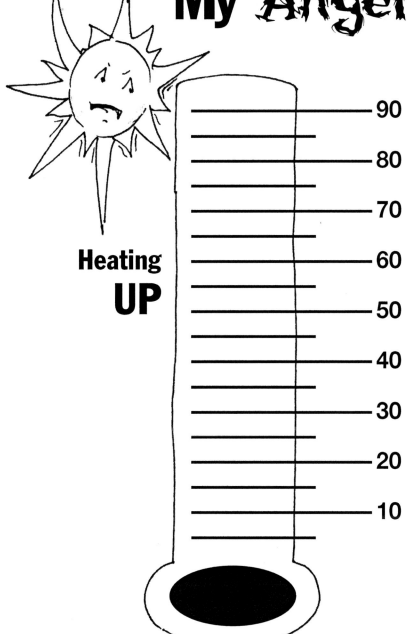

Heating
UP

- 90
- 80
- 70
- 60
- 50
- 40
- 30
- 20
- 10

Cooling
OFF

- 90
- 80
- 70
- 60
- 50
- 40
- 30
- 20
- 10

Understanding My Anger

Leader's Guide

Submitted by Sandra Christensen, BA

Purpose

To develop awareness of how we manage our anger, including what provokes anger and how families of origin have influenced our anger management.

Possible Names of Sessions

- "I Have Choices About My Anger"
- "Out with the Old, In With the New!"
- "Looking at the 'Other' Side"

Background Information

The way we handle our anger has been strongly influenced by those who raised us, yet few of us have had positive role models for handling this powerful emotion. We look at the ways our parents dealt with anger, not to blame them, but to better understand our own behavior. In order to establish new patterns in our own lives, we need to understand the old patterns that are shaping us.

Activity

1. Distribute handouts and easy-to-read pens.

2. Encourage participants to complete the sentences with the first thoughts that come to mind. Emphasize that there are no "right" or "wrong" answers.

3. Discuss the responses as a group. If your group is large, you may wish to break into smaller groups. Groups of four work best.

4. Encourage participants to share their answers to the questions, but do not force them to do so.

5. Use the discussion to make several points:

   a. Our parents (or those who raised us) play a powerful role in shaping the way we handle anger. Sometimes we have modeled ourselves on one of our parents, even if we didn't intend to. Sometimes we have selected a way of dealing with anger that is opposite of one of our parents.

   b. Although our childhood experiences influence the way we deal with anger, they do not have to determine how we deal with our anger.

   c. Most of us have more than one way of dealing with anger. We can learn to build on the positive responses and decrease the negative ones. Emphasize that change is possible!

6. Process with group members about insights gained and possible changes in anger management styles.

Variations

1. Develop a list of responses from question #6 of all the positive ways to deal with anger that were identified by group members. As participants identify particular strategies that have worked for them, ask them to share specific situations in which they have used those strategies successfully.

2. Develop a master list from responses to question #7 from the handout. Create goals based on a discussion of these with plans for follow up.

UNDERSTANDING MY ANGER

**Many of us would like to change the way we manage our anger.
Before we can establish new patterns for handling anger in our own lives,
we need to understand the old patterns that influence and shape us.**

1. One thing that really gets me angry is _____

_____

_____

2. When my mother got angry, she _____

_____

_____

3. When my father got angry, he _____

_____

_____

4. When I get angry, I _____

_____

_____

5. The people that I am closest to say my anger is

_____

_____

_____

6. One positive way I have found to deal with my anger

is to _____

_____

_____

7. One way of dealing with my anger that I would like

to change is _____

_____

_____

Am I a Worrywart?

Leader's Guide

Purpose

To explore anxiety and worry.

To get relief from anxiety and worry.

Possible Names of Sessions

- "Worrying, Where Will It Get Me?"
- "ME...A Worrywart?"
- "Looking at Anxiety...It's Time"

Background Information

Anxiety is a major health care concern for older adults. Looking at anxiety from a few different viewpoints may be helpful for gaining insight:

- sources of worry
- containing anxiety or worry
- patterns of worrying.

Activity

1. Write WORRYWART on the flipchart. Discuss the phrase and ask group members if they can identify.

2. Distribute handout and easy-to-read pens.

3. Explain to group members to complete left side and boxes at bottom of page only.

4. Review responses, commonalities and differences.

5. Ask group members to identify how worrying has had an impact on their health, relationships and lifestyle.

6. Present the idea that non-pharmaceutical methods of managing anxiety can be very useful. Explore the options of relaxation techniques, breathing, meditation, exercise, yoga, guided imagery, etc., as viable options for older adults.

7. Discuss the concept of homework.

8. Offer a few examples:

DAY	WHAT HAPPENED	WHAT YOU WORRIED ABOUT
Wed.	call from daughter	Something is wrong, someone is hurt.
Fri.	my legs are swollen	That I'm really sick.

9. Decide when homework is due.

10. After homework assignments are complete, review what patterns are noticed and what anxiety-relieving techniques were effective.

Variations

1. Lead a guided imagery exercise about putting anxiety or worries in a box.

2. Discuss and demonstrate self-talk methods or strategies that might be helpful in relieving anxiety.

Am I a Worrywart?

Do people tell you that you worry too much? Do you think you worry too much? If all your worries were taken away, would you still find something to worry about?

Let's look at your worries and put them in boxes! You can take your worries out of your boxes … any time you want.

In the last week what have you worried about …

    Getting sick?
    Losing control?
    Getting a serious illness (like Alzheimer's)?
    Failure?
    Rejection?
    Loved ones?
    Looking good?
    Other? _____

HOMEWORK: Write down when you see or find yourself worrying.

DAY	WHAT HAPPENED	WHAT YOU WORRIED ABOUT

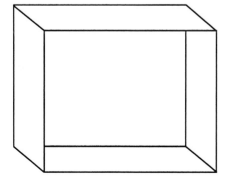 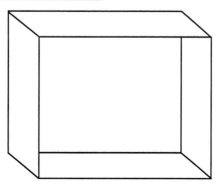 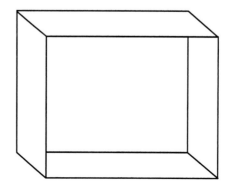 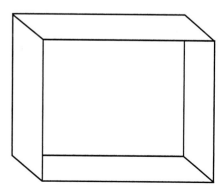

ANXIETY

Leader's Guide

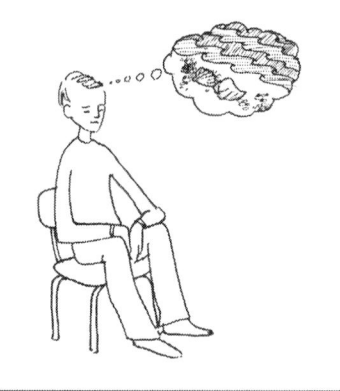

Purpose

To explore non-pharmaceutical methods of managing anxiety.

Possible Names of Sessions

- "ANXIETY...My Choices"
- "The Mind-Body Connection"
- "Breathe Away"

Background Information

Anxiety often accompanies medical and psychiatric illnesses. It can be a serious medical condition that affects all areas of functioning. Although many pharmacological means can be effective, some can have adverse side effects and be addictive.

Activity

1. Review information provided in Background Information.

2. Distribute handouts and easy-to-read pens.

3. Discuss individual symptoms and list on flipchart.

4. Explore the three relaxation possibilities each in a ten-minute practice session. After each trial, allow individuals to briefly comment and to write a personal response. Suggest that a 1-10 response before and after might be a helpful way to measure an anxiety level 1=low anxiety, 10=high anxiety.

5. Adjust each group experience to the physical limitations of the members and adapt accordingly considering hearing limitations, ROM limitations, etc.

6. Support group members in finding at least one relaxation exercise that is helpful.

7. Discuss ways that each group member can continue the most helpful methods in the future.

Variations

1. Bring in a staff member or client who has mastered any relaxation technique explored to present the benefits and lead an exercise.

2. Make audiotapes of a helpful technique for members to use in the future.

ANXIETY

Anxiety can be described as nervousness, tension, being highly-strung or exceptionally sensitive.

It is a response to fears and worries, fright and feeling overwhelmed.

Normal anxiety can be a good thing, a normal reaction to life. It can get you going. BUT WHEN THE QUALITY, INTENSITY AND DURATION IS TOO MUCH IT CAN RESULT IN **ANXIETY SYMPTOMS.**

Examples of anxiety symptoms: **Your Symptoms**

- fast breathing   _____

- muscular tension   _____

- poor memory   _____

- loss of concentration   _____

Although medications are often taken, non-pharmacological methods are also very useful! Think of the mind-body connection and try these relaxation therapy techniques.

PROGRESSIVE MUSCLE RELAXATION   Before: _____ My response after: _____

GUIDED IMAGERY   Before: _____ My response after: _____

MINDFUL BREATHING   Before: _____ My response after: _____

Leader's Guide

Submitted by Rebecca J. August, LCSW

Purpose

To gain insight into what factors go into holiday disasters and successes.

Possible Names of Sessions

- "Holidays....Are We Having Fun Yet?"
- "Hints for the Holidays"
- "Gotta Good Recipe for Surviving the Holidays?"

Background Information

For many people, holidays represent stress and unhappiness. Possible reasons include expected or unexpected expenses, seeing or spending time with relatives (or combinations of relatives), disappointments of the real vs. the ideal. It is helpful to slow down the process of the holidays and consider what works well and what doesn't.

Activity

1. Discuss the Background Information above.

2. Make a list of factors that are sure-fire "ingredients for disaster" at holiday time on the dry/erase board. Include these or develop list of your own:
   a. inviting too many people
   b. seating _____ next to _____
   c. making pies when I can buy them cheaper at the restaurant down the road
   d. being perfectionistic about the gifts, meal, house, etc.
   e. trying to do everything myself

3. Distribute handouts and easy-to-read pens.

4. Give group 10 minutes to complete left side of page.

5. Share responses.

6. Discuss that effective planning for the holidays might be a way to survive them...and even enjoy them!

7. Ask group members to complete the right side of the page and creatively complete bottom directions.

8. Share responses.

9. Encourage group members to find 'ingredients' on the right side of the page to increase the likelihood for successful holidays.

Variations

1. Write DISASTER and SURVIVAL on the board. Prepare index cards for group members to guess which category each fits in - disaster or survival. For example: Getting enough sleep, making a budget a month before, make gifts rather than buy, shop at the last minute, use credit cards.

2. Role play how to ask for help from people at holiday time.

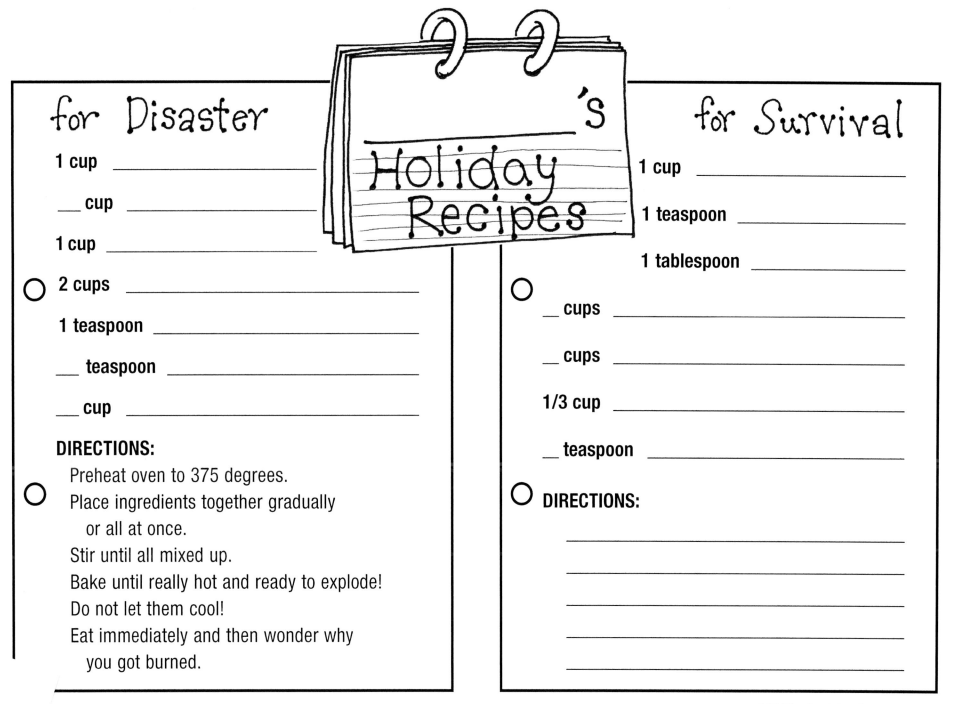

for Disaster

_____'s

Holiday Recipes

for Survival

1 cup _____

__ cup _____

1 cup _____

2 cups _____

1 teaspoon _____

__ teaspoon _____

__ cup _____

DIRECTIONS:

Preheat oven to 375 degrees.

Place ingredients together gradually
    or all at once.

Stir until all mixed up.

Bake until really hot and ready to explode!

Do not let them cool!

Eat immediately and then wonder why
    you got burned.

1 cup _____

1 teaspoon _____

1 tablespoon _____

__ cups _____

__ cups _____

1/3 cup _____

__ teaspoon _____

DIRECTIONS:

_____

_____

_____

_____

_____

STRESS RELIEF A to Z

Leader's Guide

Submitted by Wanda M. Verne, BSPM

Purpose

To explore relaxation and
stress reduction techniques.

Possible Names of Sessions

- "Reduce Your Stress –
  Alphabetically De-Stressing"
- "Create 26 New Stress Strategies"
- "The A-B-C's of Stress Management"

Background Information

When we are feeling overly stressed we
tend to forget to do the things that
ordinarily take care of ourselves – things
that we enjoy and find relaxing. Self-care is
often the first thing to go. Doing things for
ourselves breaks the cycle of our stress.
Interrupting the cycle of our stress is an
important stress management strategy.

Activity

1. Introduce the topic of stress (or anxiety) management using the background
   information. Also, discuss the importance and benefits of self-management
   strategies to overall health, relationships and quality of life.

2. Distribute handouts and easy-to-read pens.

3. Ask a volunteer to read from the left side of the page (or to make it more
   interesting, have volunteers pantomime role play each as it is read).

4. Instruct the group to develop their own STRESS RELIEF A-Z on the right side
   of the page. Encourage creativity or nonsense words for the more difficult
   letters (See the letter X).

5. Instruct group members to read their answers and discuss how this helps
   with stress relief.

Variations

1. Before the activity, discuss concept that if we always do what we have done
   in the past, we'll always get what we've gotten. Go around the room and ask
   each person, "When you're stressed out, what do you consistently do that
   never brings good results? What will happen the next time you do this?"

2. Divide group into teams of 3-4 group members. Distribute handouts and
   pencils to each team. Ask each team to complete the right side of the page.
   Give one point for each technique that no other groups list.

STRESS RELIEF A to Z

Avoid negative people   A _____

Buy yourself a flower   B _____

Call a friend   C _____

Don't know all the answers   D _____

Exercise every day   E _____

Feed the birds   F _____

Give a friend a hug   G _____

Hum a jingle   H _____

Invite a friend to dinner   I _____

Jump rope   J _____

Keep a journal   K _____

Look up at the stars   L _____

Make duplicate keys   M _____

Needlepoint a gift   N _____

Open a door for someone   O _____

Pet a friendly dog or cat   P _____

Quit trying to fix other people   Q _____

Repair things that don't work properly   R _____

Stand up and stretch   S _____

Take a bubble bath   T _____

Use time wisely   U _____

Visualize yourself relaxing   V _____

Walk in the rain   W _____

X-plore a new idea   X _____

Yawn   Y _____

Zoom into a healthy restaurant!   Z _____

Stress Symptoms

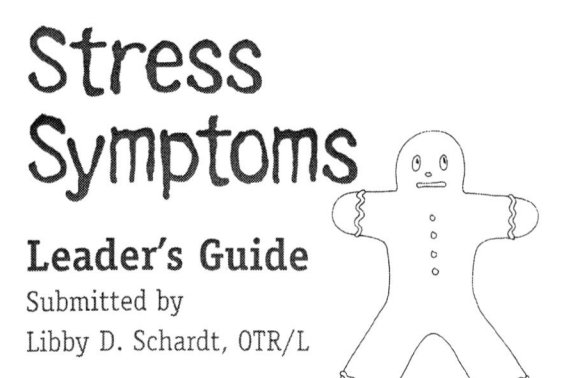

Leader's Guide

Submitted by
Libby D. Schardt, OTR/L

Purpose

To identify personal stress symptoms and positive ways to cope.

Possible Names of Sessions

- "Stress … In My Body?"
- "I FEEL My Stress"
- "Stress is in Every Body!"

Background Information

Stress can manifest itself in a variety of different symptoms. The ways that individuals deal with stress is as unique as the way it presents itself to them. This activity provides the opportunity to identify personal stress symptoms and positive ways to handle them.

Activity

1. Ask group members to define what stress is and what it means to be 'stressed out'.

2. Distribute worksheets.

3. Ask group members to circle all of the symptoms that apply to them, or occur regularly to them. Place a star next to those that occur only occasionally.

4. Discuss with group members the benefits of identifying stress symptoms and how this leads to prevention.

5. Discuss ways to handle stress and brainstorm a list. Include or add to the list:
   a. Relaxation techniques such as abdominal breathing, progressive muscle relaxation, imagery and yoga
   b. Aerobic exercise
   c. Proper diet and nutrition
   d. Cognitive restructuring-replacing negative or self-defeating thoughts with a positive gentle mind set. Replace with positive affirmations.
   e. Increase emotional expression (verbal and written)
   f. Emotional support (friends and family, counselors)
   g. Self-nurturance – take time for yourself with pleasurable activities
   h. No drugs or alcohol
   i. Develop preventative habits-priority setting and time management
   j. Learn to tolerate and forgive
   k. Stop striving for superiority – decrease perfectionism

6. Process benefits of the group.

Variations

1. Before activity, draw large human figure on flipchart. Ask group members where they feel stress in their bodies. Mark on corresponding parts of figure on flipchart.

2. Before activity, do a body check for 3 or 4 minutes. Have everyone sit with his or her eyes closed and feet flat on the floor. Name body parts that frequently are tight as a result of stress. Ask group members when it's over to identify where they carry stress in their bodies.

Stress Symptoms

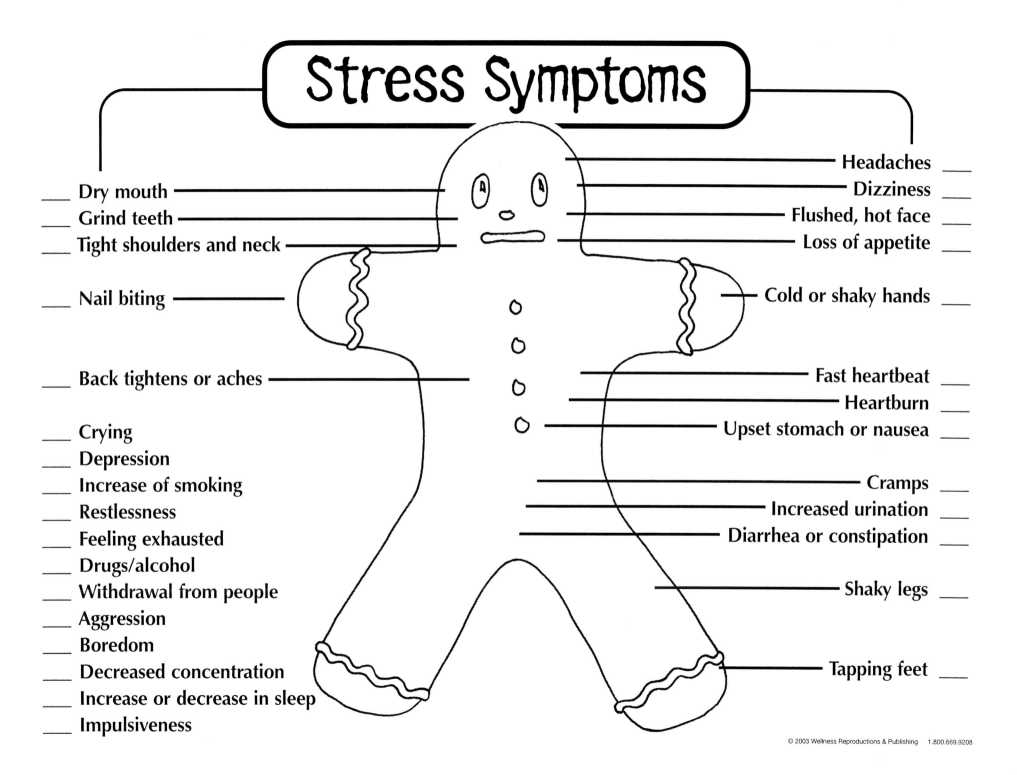

___ Dry mouth

___ Grind teeth

___ Tight shoulders and neck

___ Nail biting

___ Back tightens or aches

___ Crying

___ Depression

___ Increase of smoking

___ Restlessness

___ Feeling exhausted

___ Drugs/alcohol

___ Withdrawal from people

___ Aggression

___ Boredom

___ Decreased concentration

___ Increase or decrease in sleep

___ Impulsiveness

Headaches ___

Dizziness ___

Flushed, hot face ___

Loss of appetite ___

Cold or shaky hands

Fast heartbeat ___

Heartburn ___

Upset stomach or nausea ___

Cramps

Increased urination

Diarrhea or constipation ___

Shaky legs

Tapping feet ___

DON'T PUT ALL YOUR EGGS IN ONE BASKET!

Leader's Guide

Purpose

To establish a coping skill incorporating social supports, leisure interests, anger outlets and spiritual supports.

Possible Names of Sessions

- "An Egg-sellent Way To Cope"
- "Scramble Those Eggs!"
- "Egg-samples of a Coping Skill"

Background Information

As we age, we might naturally lose leisure interests, social and spiritual supports, and anger outlets. People move and pass away, changes occur in temples and churches, physical limitations prevent leisure, and anger outlets may diminish for a lot of different reasons. It is possible to take an active process to ensure that these important survival skills are intact.

Activity

1. Bring three baskets with four eggs in them (it might be best to hard-boiled them first). On each egg write one of the following categories: Leisure interest, social support, anger outlet and spiritual support.

2. Explain concept that if we put all our eggs in one basket and the basket gets lost, misplaced or destroyed, we would need another basket filled with the exact same things. Explain that it is possible as we age to lose supports, abilities to engage in leisure or get rid of our anger.

3. Offer example of the guy who loses the ability to play golf (due to a physical limitation). Is it probable that he lost a leisure interest, an anger outlet, and a social support? Discuss using relevant examples.

4. Distribute handouts and easy-to-read pens.

5. Divide group into pairs and instruct group members to complete handout. Give pairs an opportunity to share. If group members have eggs with nothing written on them, tell them that it's OK and there will be time for problem solving.

6. Tally results by asking, who had an egg with nothing written on it? Was it in Leisure Interests? Anger Outlets? Proceed until you can group participants by similar needs.

7. Organize large group into subgroups: People who need more anger outlets, People who need more spiritual supports, etc.

8. Allow smaller subgroups to brainstorm ideas and support each other to fill in the blanks.

9. Reconvene and share results.

Variations

1. Discuss what other categories are recommended for healthy living.

2. Serve devilled eggs as a treat at the end of the group if diets allow!

DON'T PUT ALL YOUR EGGS IN ONE BASKET!

Life often presents unexpected challenges. If we put all of our eggs in one basket, we may be disappointed or even devastated if an egg breaks, gets lost or misplaced. The 16-hour a day bicyclist who breaks his leg, the reader who loses her eyesight, the married couple who have no friends or family are examples of putting all their eggs in one basket.

You never know when an egg or two may not be available. Here are three baskets. Identify one egg from each category in EACH basket:

SOCIAL SUPPORTS, LEISURE/INTERESTS, ANGER OUTLETS, and SPIRITUAL SUPPORTS. All three baskets should have four eggs in them.

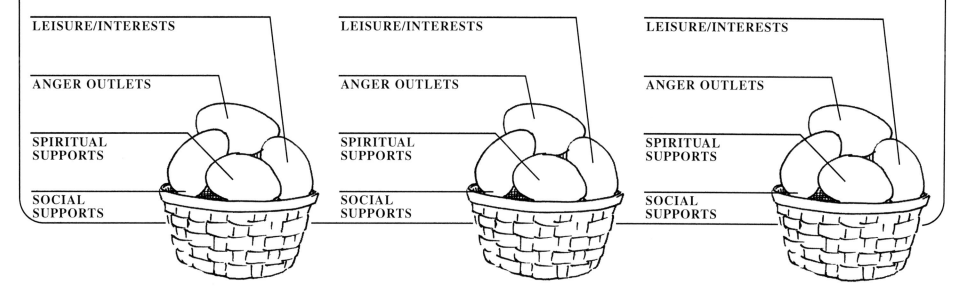

LEISURE/INTERESTS

ANGER OUTLETS

SPIRITUAL SUPPORTS

SOCIAL SUPPORTS

LEISURE/INTERESTS

ANGER OUTLETS

SPIRITUAL SUPPORTS

SOCIAL SUPPORTS

LEISURE/INTERESTS

ANGER OUTLETS

SPIRITUAL SUPPORTS

SOCIAL SUPPORTS

Making Transitions...

Leader's Guide

Submitted by Sandra Christensen, BA

Purpose

To recognize the many different feelings which accompany change.

To identify resources to help older adults positively respond to change.

Possible Names of Sessions

- "The Challenge of Change"
- "I've Never Done It This Way Before"
- "Transitions Can Be Tough!"

Background Information

Change is often a stressful part of life. Even desired changes can produce feelings of loss. By having a support system in place and developing personal coping strategies, aging adults will be better prepared to respond positively to this dynamic time of life.

Activity

1. Review background information.

2. Discuss the possible changes people in this age group might be experiencing: children or grandchildren moving away, change in job status, change in financial situation, change in the body or in physical well being, change in relationships, transition into retirement, moving from their home, etc.

3. Ask participants to complete the box on the left.

4. Encourage participants to talk about the changes they are experiencing, as well as the feelings that have accompanied those changes.

5. Transition into a discussion of the second box and encourage group members to complete. Invite participants to help each other identify resources that could assist them in responding to the changes in their lives with a positive spirit.

Variations

1. Encourage each participant to identify at least one change that has occurred in his/her lifetime, which seemed to be a negative change, but turned out to have some positive results.

2. Ask participants to talk about how their reactions to change have changed over time. What lessons have they learned over the years about how to cope with change?

Making Transitions...
smoothly and successfully

Change is an inevitable part of life. Some changes are welcome, resulting in feelings of excitement and joy. Others are unwelcome and may result in anger or despair. If you deny those unpleasant feelings, you may get "stuck" in them. By admitting your feelings and finding resources to help you cope with change, it will be easier to move forward with a positive spirit.

What changes have recently occurred in your life?

_____

_____

_____

How do you feel about those changes? List as many feeling words as you can think of to describe your reaction to the changes. _____

_____

_____

_____

_____

Check (✔) the resources you have that help you respond more positively to changes in your life?

___ family (who?) _____

___ friends (who?) _____

___ support group/counseling _____

___ a hobby (what?) _____

___ my job (paid or volunteer) _____

___ my faith community _____

___ myself! (Circle which of the following attributes help you cope with change:)

Persistence   Positive Attitude   Sense of Humor

Other: _____

___ other resources: _____

My Inner Circle

Leader's Guide

Purpose

To promote identification of supports and acknowledgement of their benefits.

Possible Names of Sessions

- "Who's There For Me?"
- "Supports Come In All Shapes and Sizes!"
- "Shape It Up!"

Background Information

It is important to take the time to see the different sources of supports in our lives. It may also be valuable (if not challenging) to assess the areas we lack support and possible reasons for this. No person can exist without the support of others; life is about giving and receiving in relationships. Having a visual reminder may serve as a lasting image of standing with others and not being alone.

Activity

1. Discuss the importance of having supports in our lives.

2. Discuss the nature of giving and receiving in relationships. Offer or elicit examples from group or look at famous well-known figures.

3. Distribute handouts and easy-to-read pens.

4. Give group members ten to fifteen minutes to complete.

5. Encourage group members to look up phone numbers in the phone book.

6. Ask each person to share his/her circle.

7. Problem solve ways of developing new supports if some shapes are empty.

Variations

1. Look at which supports were placed in certain shapes and discuss.

2. Discuss the YOUR CHOICE boxes...were there commonalities chosen? Differences?

My Inner Circle

Who is in your circle?
Think of those closest to you.
Who would you be able
to count on if you need help?

Please include the person's
name (and phone number
if you know it) in one
of the shapes:

1. A family member

2. A neighbor

3. A spiritual support or someone
   you really connect with

4. A healthcare professional

5. A 'handy' or 'helpful' person who
   knows how to get things done

6. YOUR CHOICE!

Older Adults
As Survivors and Copers

Leader's Guide

Purpose

To facilitate coping skills in older adults.

Possible Names of Sessions

- "Survival of the Fit"
- "How DO the Tough Get Going?"
- "I Have Overcome!"

Background Information

The stereotype of older adults being vulnerable and weak is perpetuated in the media and literature. As healthcare practitioners and educators we can challenge this belief by acknowledging the strengths of surviving and coping with life's adversities. Older adults may have experienced financial hard times, lack of personal choices, war, illness, and death of loved ones. Recognizing and praising a survivor attitude may be a boost for resiliency and coping skills!

Activity

1. Distribute the handouts and easy-to-read pens.

2. Ask a group member to read the top paragraph in the box with passion!

3. Give group members fifteen minutes to complete the handout.

4. Divide group into pairs.

5. Give them ten minutes to compare notes and share.

6. Reconvene and ask each group member to share one inspiration or thought shared from his or her partner.

Variations

1. Bring favorite poetry or quotes on the topic and read before or after the session.

2. Write question number eight from the handout with all comments from this question in large print on a banner or poster board. Post where staff or younger people might benefit from this wisdom.

Older Adults As Survivors and Copers

Many people consider all older adults to be vulnerable and weak. But, in fact the opposite is often true. Older adults have learned to survive. That's how they made it into their older years!

Older adults are survivors! They have coped through life's difficult and challenging times. Older adults are copers! They can cope with what life throws their way.

1. Do you feel as if you have survived tough times?
   ❏ YES ❏ NO

2. If yes, what were some tough times you can recall? _____

   _____

   _____

3. What life lessons did you learn? _____

   _____

4. What qualities or characteristics do you find in people who have overcome difficult times? _____

   _____

   _____

5. Which saying more aptly fits the way you see life? (Circle one:)

   When the going gets tough, the tough get going

   – OR –

   Life is what you make of it

6. Who is a well-known celebrity, historical figure or character in a book that you consider to be a 'survivor' or a good 'coper'? Explain. _____

   _____

   _____

   _____

7. Which is more important to you…mental toughness or physical toughness? Explain. _____

   _____

   _____

   _____

8. If you could give one piece of advice to a twenty-year-old about how best to overcome life's difficult times, what would it be? _____

   _____

   _____

   _____

STRESSORS, Coping Skills & SUPPORTS

Leader's Guide

Purpose

To assist in coping skill and support system development.

Possible Names of Sessions

- "Life Can Be Stressful...Believe It or Not!"
- "Stress...Let's Name Names!"
- "Ready or Not...Here Stress Is!"

Background Information

Coping for older adults can be challenging considering the possible lack of supports and multiple losses. Dealing with limited resources, society's myths of aging and accepting limitations can also be challenging. Recognizing coping skills might increase a sense of personal control and power. Identifying supports may decrease isolation and increase problem solving.

Activity

1. Ask group members to identify stressors that they have experienced in the last year and write them on the board for all to see.

2. Distribute handouts and easy-to-read pens.

3. Describe activity of first looking at stressors, checking them off, identifying the coping skill most likely to be used and then the support most likely to help.

4. Give group fifteen minutes to complete.

5. Share responses.

6. List all the "other" stressors, coping skills and supports.

Variations

1. Ask group members to identify and describe someone in their lives who has overcome adversity and how he or she did that.

2. Give group members blank paper. Instruct group members to divide it into three sections by folding it into thirds. Develop simple collages using pictures from magazines symbolizing stressors, coping skills and supports.

STRESSORS, Coping Skills & SUPPORTS

Getting older isn't always easy...
it can be quite stressful considering
all the possible stressors that
accompany being in this age group.

1. Consider which stressors
   you have experienced within the
   last year.

2. Check the boxes to the left of
   the **STRESSORS**. List additional
   stressors at the bottom of the list.

3. Determine which **COPING SKILL**
   best fits that stressor and write
   the matching letter on the line
   to the right.

4. Determine who is best able to
   SUPPORT you in using this skill
   effectively and write the number
   in the next line.

Stressor	Coping Skill	Support
❑ Death of a partner	_____	_____
❑ Loss of a job	_____	_____
❑ Loss of a spouse's job	_____	_____
❑ Loss of income	_____	_____
❑ Health problems	_____	_____
❑ Divorce	_____	_____
❑ Death of a loved one	_____	_____
❑ Change in activity	_____	_____
❑ Regrets about my past	_____	_____
❑ Pain	_____	_____
❑ Distant children	_____	_____
❑ Distant relatives	_____	_____
❑ Change of living environment	_____	_____
❑ Too much time	_____	_____
❑ Problems within family	_____	_____
❑ _____	_____	_____
❑ _____	_____	_____

Coping Skill Key

A. Talking
B. Books
C. Taking medications
D. Developing new interests
E. Exercising
F. Spending time alone
G. Going to temple/church
H. Spending time in nature
I. Hobbies
J. Develop a healthy routine
K. Music
L. Part-time work
M. Volunteer
N. Go out of home
O. Focus on positives
P. _____
Q. _____

Support(s) Key

1. Friend
2. Spouse
3. Neighbor
4. Clergy
5. Spirituality/ Spiritual leader
6. Children
7. Grandchildren
8. Other relatives
9. Healthcare professional
10. Group member
11. Colleague
12. Long-distance support
13. Banker
14. Community resource
15. Social group
16. _____
17. _____

Activities of Daily Living

Leader's Guide
Submitted by Regi Robnett, MS, OTR/L, BCN

Purpose

To improve insight about basic and advanced Activities of Daily Living (ADL) skills.

Possible Names of Sessions

- "The Pressure Is On"
- "Congratulations! Now Get to It!!"
- "First Things First!"

Background Information

In order to complete ADL tasks independently one must have the requisite physical, cognitive, perceptual and psychological skills to do the tasks. Older adults may have deficits in any of those areas. With mental health challenges, ADL tasks are often overlooked because of the more subtle skills: motivation and decision-making skills, planning, attention to details, social and internal cues.

This activity uses humor and discussion to focus on ADL related skills such as problem solving, time management and social appropriateness in self-care. While there are no "right" answers, the group can come to a consensus on the most important tasks, given a limited timeframe and taking into consideration a specific audience.

Activity

1. Distribute handouts and easy-to-read pens after introducing the background information to the group.

2. First as an icebreaker, ask each group member to briefly talk about (fantasize) why they might be invited to a formal dinner with the president. For example, they might
   - have a special cause (such as animal rights)
   - have a special talent which they could work on to improve, or
   - want to dedicate their lives to something they find especially meaningful.

3. Give each person the opportunity to fill out the check sheet or discuss each item, how necessary it is and how long it might take to complete.

4. Attempt to reach consensus on what needs to be done. Use a large chart or dry erase board to tally results.

5. Discuss the most relevant issues for the specific group of people:
   a. having a neat appearance and why that might or might not be important
   b. prioritizing what needs to get done before meeting others
   c. time management and how long tasks take
   d. what might make us procrastinate with our ADL tasks
   e. gender differences in ADL skills
   f. appropriate clothing/accessories for the weather, occasion, budget
   g. how to budget for ADL needs
   h. where to buy clothing and needed items
   i. individual ADL goals

6. Encourage each person to develop one goal in the area of ADL that the group could support.

Variations

1. Allow group members to prioritize and rank the most important (#1) down to the least important, having fun with even the most absurd ones.

2. Allow group members to give feedback about ADL skills (emphasizing at least one positive aspect).

ACTIVITIES OF DAILY LIVING
...What to Do First?

You have been invited to the leader of your country's house for a formal dinner tonight in honor of your contribution to your country. You only have one hour to get ready!

PRIORITIZE THE MOST IMPORTANT THINGS YOU NEED TO DO BEFORE YOU GO:

___ read the newspaper

___ go shopping for a housewarming gift

___ wash your hair

___ take a shower

___ clean your ears

___ shave (legs/face)

___ cut your fingernails/ get a manicure

___ feed the dog

___ pluck your nose hairs

___ gargle

___ scrub the toilet

___ polish your shoes

___ apply make up/aftershave

___ iron your clothes

___ use deodorant

___ floss your teeth

___ unplug the iron

___ drink carrot juice

___ try on several outfits

___ eat a snack

___ call a friend

___ dye your hair

___ dress in appropriate clothing

___ find clothes on the floor to wear

___ use a mud mask

___ rub limberger cheese on body

___ Other: _____

___ Other: _____

___ Other: _____

Keeping On Schedule

Leader's Guide

Purpose

To offer an organizational tool to make sure that meaningful activities happen when they are scheduled.

Possible Names of Sessions

- "Making Sure It Happens"
- "What's to Do in a Week?"
- "Organizing My Life...
  so no one else needs to!!!"

Background Information

Responsibilities can easily be overwhelming to all of us, including appointments, exercise programs, vitamins, medications, calls to make, home maintenance, activities with children and grandchildren, paying bills, etc, etc, etc! It can become burdensome and stressful just thinking about it. Checklists serve as a way to organize information and a way of setting up a self-accountability schedule.

Activity

1. Distribute one handout to each individual and an easy-to-read pen.

2. List on the board all of the things that group members do in a day. This list may include: taking medications (over-the-counter or prescription), exercises, appointments, telephone calls, visits, health care activities (taking blood pressure, listening to relaxation tapes) and meetings.

3. Check off the activities that group members identify that they have difficulty remembering.

4. Explain that this handout serves as an organizational tool for those activities.

5. Give group members ten minutes to complete the handout.

There are a few ways to use this handout:

a. One activity for a month: e.g. Take Tegretol 3 times a day. Then, instruct the group members to place three checks (✓) in each day's box. ONCE THE ACTIVITY IS ACCOMPLISHED, IT GETS A BACKWARDS SLASH THROUGH THE CHECK (✗). Some people might find writing the date below the day of the week helpful.

b. Use as a weekly guide with non-everyday responsibilities. Instruct group members to write in four activities for the week: e.g., call my therapist and ask a question (T), do my leg exercises (MWF), baby-sit the grandkids (Tu and Th), water the plants (Su).

c. Collaborate and develop another system individualized for the people in the session.

6. Ask each person to share his/her completed handout with the group.

Variations

1. Develop a few fictitious checklists before the group of hypothetical schedules that might assist this group.

2. Use this handout with other handouts that will reinforce follow through of an activity.

Keeping On Schedule

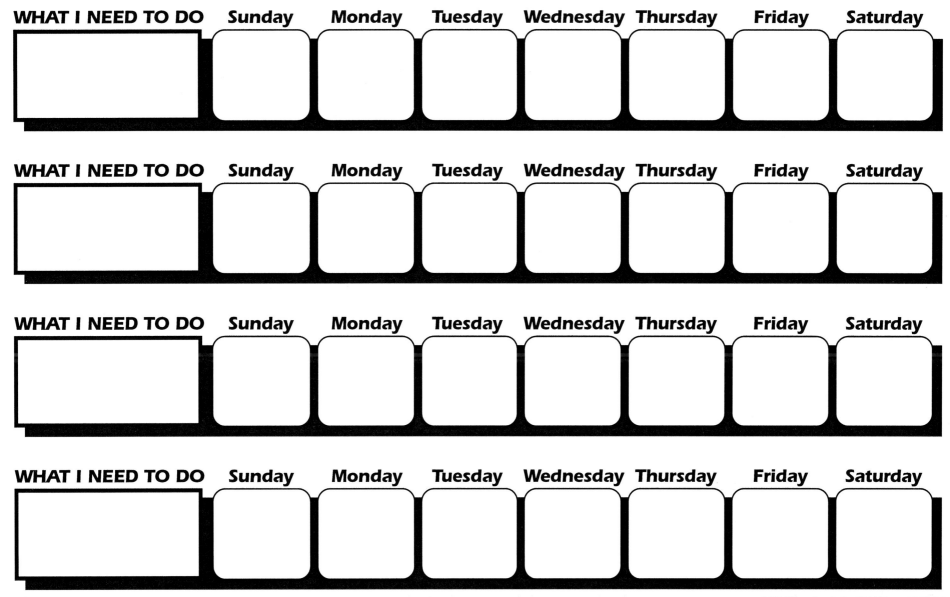

WHAT I NEED TO DO | Sunday | Monday | Tuesday | Wednesday | Thursday | Friday | Saturday

WHAT I NEED TO DO | Sunday | Monday | Tuesday | Wednesday | Thursday | Friday | Saturday

WHAT I NEED TO DO | Sunday | Monday | Tuesday | Wednesday | Thursday | Friday | Saturday

WHAT I NEED TO DO | Sunday | Monday | Tuesday | Wednesday | Thursday | Friday | Saturday

Morning Routine

Leader's Guide

Submitted by Melissa L. Oliver, OTR/L, MS
and Vicki L. Addison, COTA

Purpose

To develop a morning routine
with the assistance of a checklist.

Possible Names of Sessions

- "Up and Moving in the Right Direction!"
- "Morning Routine Gets the Day Going"
- "No Excuses Now!"

Background Information

Morning routines often get interrupted due
to illness, trauma or flare-up of a disability.
Visual reminders such as checklists provide
prompts for individuals to reestablish
functional routines. The Morning Routine
chart offers cues to initiate and complete
difficult-to-do morning activities of
daily living.

Activity

1. Introduce and explain purpose for checklist.

2. Distribute handouts, easy-to-read pens and highlighters.

3. Give group members five to ten minutes to review list on left and highlight those that individuals need to do in the morning.

4. Ask group members to identify additional tasks to be listed under "Other". List on board.

5. Explain to group that the purpose is to review first thing in the morning. The list can be checked as each task is completed or after they have "completed" the morning routine. At this point, they can review list and see the unchecked boxes. Checklists can be used on an ongoing basis or discontinued as morning routine is re-established.

6. Explore possible locations for the checklist to be hung in the home.

Variations

1. Laminate the checklists and use dry erase markers for re-use or offer additional photocopied checklists for continued use.

2. Use the handouts as part of a treatment plan monitoring how much independence it takes to successfully complete tasks.

Morning Routine

CHECK THE FOLLOWING ITEMS:

	SUNDAY	MONDAY	TUESDAY	WEDNESDAY	THURSDAY	FRIDAY	SATURDAY
Go to the bathroom							
Wash hands							
Take bath or shower							
Shave							
Brush hair							
Brush teeth or clean dentures							
Put on deodorant							
Get dressed							
Put make-up on							
Make bed							
Take medication							
Fix breakfast							
Eat breakfast							
Other: _____							

Quick Picks...
for the Week

Leader's Guide
Submitted by Martin B. Golub, CTRS

Purpose

To identify tasks to do for the week.

To identify leisure/social activities to do for the week.

To organize one's time better.

Possible Names of Sessions

- "Balancing Responsibilities with FUN!"
- "How Can I Fit It All In"
- "Planning for Success"

Background Information

Part of being an independent person is the ability to structure and plan one's week and to organize one's time. This handout assists people in identifying what they need to get done for the week.

Activity

1. Discuss the benefits of planning one's weekly tasks, chores and leisure. The group may develop a list.

2. On a flipchart or dry erase board have the group devise a list of possible tasks, chores and responsibilities. Discuss the importance of doing these tasks, e.g., keeping the apartment organized, not letting things build up which can be stressful, having clean clothes.

3. Now, list possible leisure/social activities for the week. Discuss the importance of having leisure and social activities, e.g., enjoying others company and having a support system, being an interesting person, humor supports the immune system.

4. Distribute handouts and easy-to-read pens.

5. Give ample time to complete. Share results. Discuss challenges and how to overcome obstacles.

6. Discuss where this list can be placed so that it can be easily reviewed.

Variations

1. Use on Monday mornings and repeat for several weeks to help people get used to planning their weeks. After the first time, this handout can be used as a warm-up or starter activity for a group session.

2. Encourage people to write the day of the week for each chosen task/activity. (M=Monday, T-Tuesday, W=Wednesday, TH=Thursday, F=Friday, SA=Saturday, SU=Sunday)

Quick Picks... for the Week

"Quick Pick" what you would like to get done this week. Write in specifics if you'd like. Circle what you want to accomplish.

RESPONSIBILITIES

Household Chores

Community Errands

Room Cleaning

Straightening Up

Cooking

Things to Buy

Grocery Shopping

Banking

Balance Checkbook

Appointments

Laundry

Bills to Pay

Other Chores / Responsibilities _____

LEISURE / SOCIAL

Visit with Family

Write Notes or Emails

Read Articles or Books

Call Friends

Watch Shows or Movies

Go Fun or Enjoyable Places

Visit People

Walk

Do Hobbies

Play Cards or Games

Listen to Music

Exercise

Other Leisure / Social _____

Same old, same old? Not for long!

Leader's Guide

Purpose

To increase meaningful activities and the quality of life.

Possible Names of Sessions

- "Keep It Interesting"
- "All Work and No Play..."
- "Always Ready for a Challenge"

Background Information

There might be a tendency to stick to old routines and expectations, which in turn may lead to a rigid routine and inflexibility. The result is oftentimes boredom, isolation and a depressed mood. New activities may...introduce a new social group, provide exciting challenges, offer different ideas and elicit interesting conversations! In addition, it may take the place of sedentary or nonproductive activities.

Activity

1. Introduce concept by reviewing background information. It might be helpful to get a sense of the group members activity level by asking thought-provoking questions like, "How many hours of TV do you generally watch a day?" "When was the last time you tried a new food?"

2. Distribute handouts and easy-to-read pens.

3. Ask a group member to read aloud the top portion.

4. Give group members ten minutes to complete the handouts.

5. Briefly review results by asking how many checked "trying new foods", "doing a new sport", etc.

6. Pair group members of similar interests to discuss plans for five minutes.

7. Reconvene and ask group members to share interesting plans and ideas.

Variations

1. Develop goals, accountability and a method for reporting back to the group progress that has been made.

2. Bring a new food (easy snack, exotic fruit, etc) to the group as an intro and process the results!

Same old, same old? Not for long!

Although there is great value to keeping a daily routine, there is also value to trying new activities. Change can be good and it helps us to be fun and interesting people. New activities can help us feel alive and challenged!

Read below and check the three activities that are the most appealing to you. Then complete the second column by answering who could be helpful or supportive. Now, write in the third column the next step for doing this new activity.

Step New Activity	Who Could Be Helpful or Supportive?	What's the Next in Doing This?
❏ Trying a new food	_____	_____
❏ Doing a new sport or exercise	_____	_____
❏ Traveling	_____	_____
❏ Taking a course or class	_____	_____
❏ Getting together with a new friend	_____	_____
❏ Volunteering	_____	_____
❏ Becoming involved in politics	_____	_____
❏ Joining a club	_____	_____
❏ Going to a new place in your community	_____	_____
❏ _____	_____	_____
❏ _____	_____	_____

Slow and Steady Wins the Race

Leader's Guide

Purpose

To set daily and weekly goals.

Possible Names of Sessions

- "Keep on Chugging!"
- "Sharing the Goal"
- "Daily & Weekly Goals"

Background Information

Goals can further our intentions. We often think we want to do something – sometimes we tell someone, and sometimes we don't. Sometimes stating a goal can make the action piece come alive. Including supportive people in the goals we set can get the help to accomplish goals, improve relationships and reduce possible isolation.

Activity

1. Write on the flipchart all the possible areas in which we can set daily goals: Eating, taking care of our bodies, housekeeping, friendships, calls to make, activities to engage in, etc.

2. Explain that a goal is a statement that can be written and crossed off when accomplished. It is not a dream that can't be crossed off, e.g., To be happy, To be a good friend.

3. Distribute handouts and easy-to-read pens.

4. Give one or two examples of goals and people with whom we can share goals, e.g., By the end of the day, I will call my sister. I can share this goal with my neighbor. By the end of the day, I will clean my bedroom. I will share this goal with my case manager.

5. Give group members ten minutes to develop personal goals.

6. Share in groups of three or four, asking group members to support and give feedback.

7. Ask group members to share their favorite goals and list on flipchart for all to see.

Variations

1. Develop a way of checking with group members to see if goals were accomplished. (Notebook, flipchart)

2. Discuss possibility of self-reward when goals are accomplished and bring reward to individuals or group if appropriate.

Slow and Steady Wins the Race

Remember the story of the tortoise and the hare? The tortoise won...
with determination, persistence and a not-giving-up attitude.

Realistic goals keep us moving in a positive direction, towards good health and the ability to do what we want to do and when and how we want to do it. Sharing our goals with others can help us stick to them.

By the end of the day, I will _____

_____ .

I can share this goal with _____ .

By the end of the day, I will _____

_____ .

I can share this goal with _____ .

By the end of the week, (_____), I will _____

_____ .

I can share this goal with _____ .

Effects of Emotional Abuse

Leader's Guide

Submitted by
Esterlee A. Molyneux, MS, SSW

Purpose

To identify some of the effects a victim suffers from being exposed to emotional abuse.

Possible Names of Sessions

- "Searching for the Truth about Emotional Abuse"

- "The Aftermath of Emotional Abuse"

- "What Is Emotional Abuse, Anyway?"

Background Information

Too often people are unaware of the toll that emotional abuse places on their lives. People who are emotionally abusive may not realize the long-term consequences as well. This activity is meant to bring to light some of the effects of emotional abuse for both the abuser and the one being abused.

Activity

1. Define what emotional abuse is: a pattern of behavior that retards a person's sense of self-development.

2. Explain that people who have been abused repeatedly report that out of all forms of abuse, emotional abuse is the most difficult to overcome.

3. Distribute handouts and highlighters or easy-to-read pens.

4. Give participants ample time to complete the word search. Explain that the words they are searching for are all possible effects of emotional abuse. Instruct the group members that words can be found forward, backward, upward, downward, diagonal or backwards and diagonal.

5. Discuss using explanations below. Give examples of how each effect could be a result of emotional abuse.

    BLAMES - the person who is abused often blames others for the poor choices s/he makes because s/he was blamed by the abuser for mistakes s/he didn't make

    COLD - those who have been emotionally abused can become cold and insensitive to others' feelings because that's how they were treated. They have learned to respond to others in the same way.

    COMPULSIVE - compulsive behaviors may arise from being exposed to repeated emotional abuse

    DEPRESSED - in an emotionally abusive relationship, depression is a common side effect due to the negative, unyielding and unhopeful environment

    DESTRUCTIVE - the pain that those emotionally abused suffer inside can be so intense that they find destructive ways such as self-mutilation, substances or suicide attempts to try and rid themselves of the pain

    FAILURE - those who have been emotionally abused have been told in words and/or actions that they are generally worthless. This can lead one to feel like s/he is unable to succeed.

    GUILTY -people who have experienced emotional abuse can feel like the abuse is their fault and feel guilty for "provoking" the abuser

    INSECURE - those who have been abused often find they don't have a 'safe place' to vent feelings and share concerns, not feeling secure in the world

    LACK OF TRUST - victims of emotional abuse can become untrusting of those around them because they do not know if and when the abuser will 'explode' and when they will become the target of aggression

    LOW SELF-ESTEEM - after repeatedly hearing negative comments, self-esteem gets diminished

    NEGATIVE SELF-TALK - when individuals hear repeatedly what horrible people they are, they start to believe it and perpetuate the abuse by putting themselves down

    NO VALUE - people who have been emotionally abused often feel like they are undeserving and have no value

    PASSIVE - the abused person often learns to be submissive to the abuse and is afraid to stand up for his/her rights

    RAGE - rage can build up inside of those abused, because they feel angry about what is happening to them

    REJECTING - due to the abuse, persons who have been abused can reject any positive comment or compliment because they do not feel worthy

    SHY - those abused may feel shy or timid around people for several reasons such as low self-worth, feelings of being undeserving of friends, and afraid that another may find out how things really operate in their home

    SLEEP DISORDERS - nightmares, sleep disturbances, etc., can be a result of emotional abuse

    SPEECH DISORDERS - emotional abuse takes its toll on the brain and can result in learning disorders, including speech disorders

    SUBSTANCE ABUSE - to escape the pain from emotional abuse, many victims turn to drugs or alcohol to help them escape temporarily from the reality that they are facing

    ULCERS - emotional abuse results in stress which can give one ulcers

    UNWORTHY - those abused often feel unworthy of love or attention from others due to the pattern of interaction they have with the perpetrator

    WEAK - those abused can feel weak particularly around the abuser feeling they have no control

Variations

1. Review explanations listed above as a separate group session.

2. Invite a professional to come in to the next session to discuss "What to Do If You Are Living in an Emotionally Abusive Situation". Inform group members that emotionally abusive relationships might include parent-child, grandparent-grandchild, spouse-spouse, landlord-tenant or other combinations.

Effects of Emotional Abuse

```
Y  S  E  S  U  B  A  E  C  N  A  T  S  B  U  S
H  S  T  D  D  E  S  T  R  U  C  T  I  V  E  A
T  R  H  R  R  S  R  E  J  E  C  T  I  N  G  D
S  E  N  Y  E  S  E  W  L  S  S  R  E  C  L  U
U  D  O  O  J  I  D  M  U  I  P  E  U  O  O  M
R  R  V  S  P  V  R  A  A  V  C  N  B  M  W  R
T  O  A  I  G  A  O  K  C  L  W  W  Y  P  S  L
F  S  L  G  A  W  S  U  L  O  B  T  W  U  E  E
O  I  U  D  E  I  I  S  R  E  L  N  C  L  L  R
K  D  E  A  N  A  D  T  I  I  U  D  E  S  F  U
C  P  K  E  B  F  H  C  U  V  S  F  G  I  E  C
A  E  D  S  C  Y  C  G  P  B  E  I  H  V  S  E
L  E  E  S  L  O  E  R  U  L  I  A  F  E  T  S
K  L  A  T  F  L  E  S  E  V  I  T  A  G  E  N
P  S  E  S  W  O  P  O  M  A  E  J  G  N  E  I
R  D  E  P  R  E  S  S  E  D  M  R  J  O  M  K
```

BLAMES
COLD
COMPULSIVE
DEPRESSED
DESTRUCTIVE
FAILURE
GUILTY
INSECURE
LACK OF TRUST
LOW SELF ESTEEM
NEGATIVE SELF-TALK
NO VALUE
PASSIVE
RAGE
REJECTING
SHY
SLEEP DISORDERS
SPEECH DISORDERS
SUBSTANCE ABUSE
ULCERS
UNWORTHY
WEAK

Emotions Plus

Leader's Guide

Purpose

To facilitate emotions expression.

To recognize the benefits of emotion expression.

Possible Names of Sessions

- "Speaking the Unspoken...EMOTIONS!"
- "Feelings For a Lifetime"
- "Better Out Than In!"

Background Information

Expressing feelings can be quite a challenge! To know what we are feeling and then to be able to find the right word to express it to others is a lifelong skill. Oftentimes we live life with feelings stirring below the surface but can't find the language. The thirty-five emotion words listed on this handout are commonly felt but are sometimes difficult to express.

Activity

1. Write on the board, "How Are You Feeling?"
2. Ask group members to name what they typically hear as a response: "fine", "OK", "good".
3. Explain to the group that this session is about expanding the vocabulary and skill of emotion expression.
4. Ask group members about the consequences or implications of NOT expressing emotions, e.g. impaired relationships, ulcers, high blood pressure, risky behaviors. Consider relevant answers exploring the body-mind connection.
5. Distribute handouts with easy-to-read pens.
6. Explain that emotions rarely come one at a time. We often feel emotions simultaneously. Also, emotions are not negative or positive; instead they can be viewed as comfortable and uncomfortable. Expressing uncomfortable feelings may be difficult, but will lead to a healthier lifestyle and growth.
7. Ask each group member to circle one comfortable emotion and one uncomfortable emotion felt in the last few days.
8. First, give everyone an opportunity to express the comfortable emotion in a structured, simple format: "I feel _____ when _____ or I felt _____ when _____." For example, I feel relieved when the doctor gives me a clean bill of health. I felt satisfied when I was enjoying time with my grandkids yesterday.
9. Then do the same with uncomfortable emotions. For example, I felt jealous when I went to Sally's house and saw her so happy with her family. I feel helpless when I try to move quickly in the morning and can't. _____
10. Encourage group members to post the handout in a visible place where it can be referred to easily.

Variations

1. Explore if there is a relationship between early messages we received about emotion expression by the people who raised us, and how we express emotions today.
2. Create a *How I Feel Today* collage with magazine cutouts, using the handout as a guide.

Resource Note

Corresponding EMOTIONS PLUS, 24" x 36" color poster available. Call 1.800.669.9208 for a catalogue, or see order form in back of book.

Emotions Plus
a Lifetime of Feelings

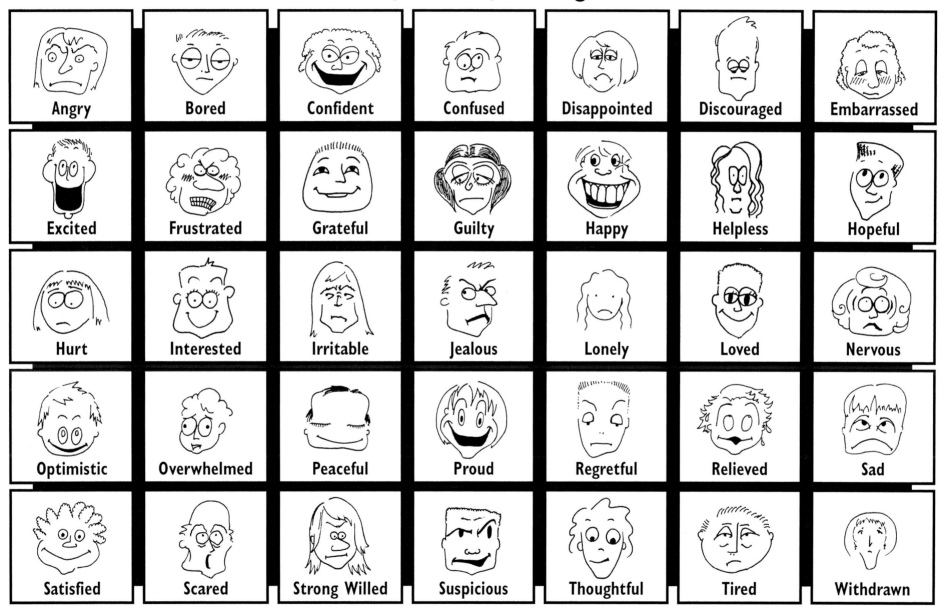

Angry	Bored	Confident	Confused	Disappointed	Discouraged	Embarrassed
Excited	Frustrated	Grateful	Guilty	Happy	Helpless	Hopeful
Hurt	Interested	Irritable	Jealous	Lonely	Loved	Nervous
Optimistic	Overwhelmed	Peaceful	Proud	Regretful	Relieved	Sad
Satisfied	Scared	Strong Willed	Suspicious	Thoughtful	Tired	Withdrawn

If I Could Write a Book...

Leader's Guide

Submitted by Mark S. Macko, MEd

Purpose

To increase emotional expression and disclosure.

Possible Names of Sessions

- "It's Time to Tell Your Story"
- "My Book Would Be About..."
- "The Chapters of My Life... Read All About It"

Background Information

The ability to self-disclose has direct bearing on an individual's potential for recovery and self-discovery. Using incomplete sentence stems or starters, facilitates such disclosure, while incorporating an activity that condenses a person's life story. This creative alternative to verbal emotional expression can easily be a launching pad to interesting verbal expression.

Activity

1. Begin group by discussion of 'writing one's memoirs'. Remind each group member that although only a small percentage of people actually write a book about themselves – everyone's life story is interesting, unique and worth telling.

2. Distribute handouts and pens.

3. Encourage participants to complete the sentence stems. Explain that there are no right or better responses, only different ones, since each person in the group is a special person with his / her story to tell.

4. Elicit responses from group members by :
   a) asking each sentence stem at a time for each person or
   b) having each participant respond to all of the sentence stems.

5. Expound on specific sentence stems. Explore reasons for what each group member would delete (if any), why a certain chapter would be more difficult to write, or the meaning behind the individual titles of books. Group facilitator could expound upon any sentence stem.

6. Begin group discussion about writing memoirs, providing benefits and values of doing so, e.g., "If it's not written down, it will be lost", "Each person has his / her own story to tell", "No one has a journey just like you", encouraging group members to get started!

Variations

1. Talk about proposed benefits of journalizing, e.g., as a way to relieve tension, having a companion who is always available, an alternative means of emotional expression, a way of healing. Discuss the different forms of journalizing. Determine who has kept a journal (or diary) in the past, why they stopped, who is considering keeping one again, or for the first time. Remind members that they do not have to tell their life story, only take 'one day at a time' to express their thoughts and emotions.

2. Create new sentence stems with group members, write on board and give everyone an opportunity to respond. Examples might include:
   My Thank You page would include _____ .
   The cover of my book would look like _____ .

If I Could Write a Book...

It would begin with ...

_____

The easiest chapter would be ...

_____

I would leave out the part about ...

_____

My most difficult chapter would be ...

_____

I would let _____ read it.
   (Specify: anyone, a few, no one)

I _would / would not_ include information
about all my family members. (circle)

My book would be
more fact / more fiction.   (circle)

The longest chapter would be ...

_____

The shortest chapter would be ...

_____

My book would be
very long / very short.   (circle)

A possible title for my book would be ...

_____

I would dedicate my book to ...

_____

I _will / will not_ write a book about my life.
   (circle)

The last book I read about someone was ...

_____

The Emotions Balloon

Leader's Guide

Submitted by
Rick Germann, MA, LCPC, RPRP

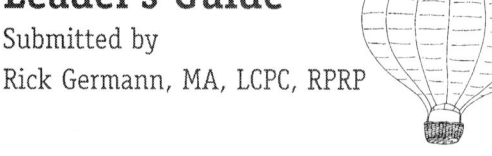

Purpose

To understand one's level of emotions in response to real-life situations.

Possible Names of Sessions

- "Up, Up and Away!"
- "Uplifting Emotions"
- "When Does Your Balloon Burst?"

Background Information

Each person is created in a unique way and, as a result, will emotionally respond to situations differently. What produces a high level of emotion, such as anger, in one person – may produce very little in another. Taking the time and effort to think about our responses in a safe setting as well as explore the way we deal with them will give insight and opportunity for change.

Activity

1. Introduce the concept of having a 'threshold' for emotions and how using a balloon can depict this. A balloon can only hold a certain quantity of air before it will burst, just as a person who holds too much emotional energy may 'burst'.

2. Distribute handouts with pencils, markers or other coloring utensils.

3. Inform the group that you will be describing a series of real-life situations that may produce emotions in people. Examples might be:
   - A surprise party is thrown in your honor.
   - A tax refund arrives.
   - Your granddaughter unexpectedly states s/he will be having a baby.
   - Water damage happens to your home/apartment.
   - Your significant other comes home two hours late with no explanation.

4. With each situation, ask group members to color in the balloon in relation to the amount of emotion they would experience in this situation.

5. After a series of situations are discussed (be careful not to come up with too many or everyone's balloon will 'pop'!), ask the group members to show their balloons and discuss which situations caused them to color the most of the balloon.

6. Process by discussing ways of releasing some of the air from the balloon to guard against 'bursting'.

Variations

1. Give each group member a balloon (make sure you always use new balloons for sanitary reasons) and inform them that you will be describing a series of real-life situations that may produce emotions in people. With each situation the group members are to think about how emotional this would make them and then to blow an amount of air into their balloon to represent their emotions.

2. Distribute seven handouts to each group member (or correspond the number with the amount of days until you will meet with the group again). Ask them to record their real-life situations with colored-in spaces in their balloons. For example a small red blob has 'bill collector called' written in it, a large blue blob has 'dog ran away' written in it. Discuss in next session.

The Emotions Balloon

My rights as an older adult...

Leader's Guide

Purpose

To address the emotional needs and rights of an older adult.

Possible Names of Sessions

- "What Do You Need?"
- "Tough Things To Talk About?"
- "Recognizing My Rights"

Background Information

Being an older adult isn't always easy. The older adults' specific needs and rights are oftentimes overlooked and sometimes ignored. Feeling alive and good about who they are, what they can contribute, and feeling valuable are highlighted in this handout. It will hopefully enhance communication, healthy interactions and promote positive, supportive relationships.

Activity

1. Explain background information.

2. Distribute handouts and easy-to-read pens.

3. Discuss each item, allowing group members to raise concerns about specific rights.

4. Instruct group members to check the boxes of the rights that relate to them.

5. Allow for further ideas to be shared from the others section on the bottom right.

6. Divide group into pairs to allow for problem solving to approach these issues.
   Is it best to discuss these issues *directly* with the person involved? What are strategies for direct communication of this nature? Is it best to discuss them *indirectly*? If indirectly, what are some methods?

   For example, referring to the numbers on the front of the handout:
   3. speaking in a volume you can hear
   4. thanking the person when s/he is patient
   10. asking someone to brush your hair and then telling them it felt good

7. Reconvene and share results of work shared in pairs.

Variations

1. Role play one direct and one indirect method of communication with each of the ten rights.

2. Videotape the role plays with older adults' written and verbal permission for future presentations.

My rights as an older adult...

**As an older adult – I would like to ask for the following courtesies,
allowing me to live the rest of my life with honor, dignity and respect.**

(Check the following as they apply to you – and add in your own words in the blank lines, if you like)

❑ 1. Talk to me as if I am an adult. _____
_____

❑ 2. I want to feel as if I can still do certain things
(even if I am becoming more dependent than I used
to be). _____
_____

❑ 3. I want to hear you. Talk loud enough (without
screaming or talking too slowly) so I won't need to
ask you to repeat. _____
_____

❑ 4. Try to be patient – I am trying! _____
_____

❑ 5. My sense of humor is still there – have fun with me!
_____
_____

❑ 6. Try and make sense of what I am saying. _____
_____

❑ 7. Be present when you're with me. Really listen.
_____
_____

❑ 8. De-emphasize limitations and shortcomings I can't
do anything about. _____
_____

❑ 9. Touch me physically in a safe and loving way. ____
_____

❑ 10. I have the right to be in healthy relationships and
not be subjected to physical, sexual, financial or
emotional abuse. _____
_____

OTHERS

❑ _____
_____

❑ _____
_____

❑ _____
_____

Reveal How You Feel

Leader's Guide

Submitted by Kimberly D. Heath, MA

Purpose

To uncover and share one's true feelings.

Possible Names of Sessions

- "Mirror, Mirror…"
- "What's Under the Mask?"
- "Zorro, Superman and Me…
  What Do We Have in Common?"

Background Information

Knowing how we feel and being able to express those true feelings can help us improve the quality of our lives. Too often we wear "masks" that reveal to others what we think they want to see or what we want them to see. By pretending how we feel, we are denying ourselves the opportunity to be ourselves, to connect with others and to make progress.

Activity

1. Discuss how difficult it is to reveal what's really going on in our lives. Briefly list a few possible obstacles, e.g., there is a fear that if people saw the real me, they would be scared, they won't like me, and wouldn't think the same of me.

2. Distribute handouts and markers.

3. Ask the group to draw the mask that they put on for others, in the mirror on the left. Discuss why they wear this mask.

4. Ask the group members to draw a picture of how they really feel in the mirror on the right side. Discuss what it would be like to have others see their true feelings.

5. Ask the group members to give each other feedback regarding the mask vs. the true expression of feelings.

6. Discuss the impact of both masks and true emotion expression.

Variations

1. Pair group members. Ask group member A to draw how they see group member B, in the mirror on the left. Ask group member B to draw how they see group member A, in the mirror on the left. Then, ask group members to trade papers and draw how they could be seen, without a mask, in the mirror on the right.

2. After both mirrors are finished, gather handouts for everyone to see and look for similarities and differences. Factors to look for might include gender, ethnic background, age, culture, etc.

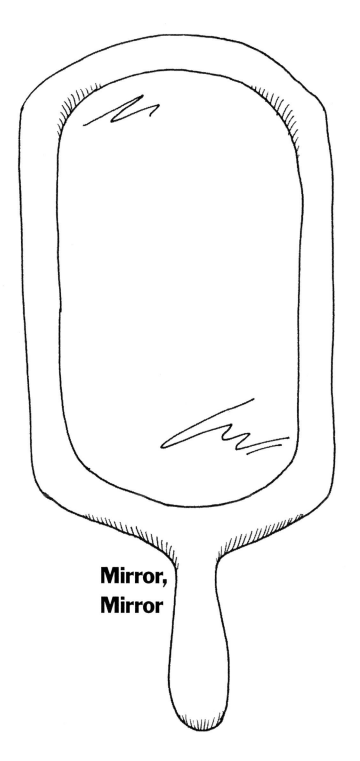

Reveal How You Feel

Mirror, Mirror

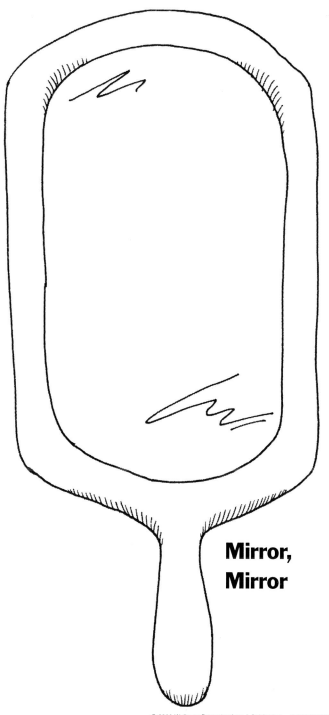

Mirror, Mirror

Grief Grabs You

Leader's Guide

Purpose

To facilitate the grief process by:
1) acknowledging often unrecognized symptoms and feelings, and 2) recognizing benefits of discussing grief in a group setting.

Possible Names of Sessions

- "Dealing with Grief in a Group"
- "My Grief...Your Grief"
- "Feeling My Grief? Not ME!"

Background Information

Grief is an intense feeling of deep sorrow and sadness caused by a loss. Oftentimes when people are experiencing grief symptoms, they are feeling alone, isolated and unsupported. It is important for people who are grieving to realize that they are not alone and that there are common grief symptoms and feelings.

Activity

1. Present concept of grief "grabbing" a person when s/he least expects it.

2. Ask group members to complete handouts by identifying which situations happen to them.

3. Discuss each situation, asking members to volunteer to share their experiences.

4. Pursue *other* comments, asking group members to share what they wrote.

5. Discuss last thought on the bottom of the page, *it'll get better...and if not better, it'll get different*. Ask members if they've noticed a difference as time has passed.

6. Process the benefits of recognizing grief symptoms and feelings, and discussing grief in a group setting.

Variations

1. Discuss each situation listed on the handout, asking a group member to volunteer to share an emotion that co-exists with grief in that particular situation. Assist group members by using a list of varied emotions. (See page 26, *Emotions Plus* or *Emotions Plus* poster. Refer to order form on back page.)

2. Write 'What Has Helped' on the board. Ask group members to name those things that have helped in the grief process and list on board. List may include: people listening to me, getting a good night's sleep, talking to others who have lost someone, being outdoors.

Grief Grabs You
when you're least prepared!

Do You:

☐ feel lonely even though you are in a room filled with people?

☐ feel overwhelmed with the flooding of many emotions?

☐ forget what you were about to do 5 minutes ago?

☐ try to go to sleep and see "replays"?

☐ have a difficult time concentrating?

☐ have a sense of being incomplete?

☐ cry for no apparent reason?

☐ feel cheated?

☐ feel a twang when you see a striking resemblance, a familiar hairdo, certain clothing?

☐ feel like staying in bed, or better yet, climbing under the bed?

☐ find it hard to imagine that others' lives go on? people are still laughing? the sun still shines?

☐ wish your loved one, who is no longer in your life, could see your children, see what you are accomplishing, etc.?

☐ feel fine for a period of time, and get depressed again for no apparent reason?

☐ feel angry at your loved one whom you've lost, yourself, your family, or people who are trying to help you?

☐ other _____

☐ other _____

☐ other _____

Do You Feel Saddened When:

☐ you smell a familiar cologne, shaving cream, etc.?

☐ you go to a religious ceremony? meaningful event?

☐ it's the anniversary date of a birthday? wedding? death? divorce?

☐ you see the beauty of everything coming alive in spring? the leaves turning color in fall?

☐ you see a couple arm-in-arm?

☐ you see a father and son, mother and daughter, siblings, best friends, etc. together?

☐ you hear a certain song? certain type of music?

☐ other _____

☐ other _____

☐ other _____

☐ other _____

...it'll get better...and if not better, it'll get different!

Inside Outside

Leader's Guide

Purpose

To gain insight regarding the discrepancy between how one feels and what one expresses while experiencing grief.

To identify:
1) the implications of the "Inside, I Feel..." / "Outside, I Appear..." discrepancy, and
2) ways to bridge the gap of this discrepancy.

Possible Names of Sessions

- "It's What I'm NOT Telling You!"
- "Grief...Gets In the Way"
- "Masking My Feelings"

Background Information

Oftentimes, people in grief feel that no one understands them. They often don't understand themselves. It might be due to discrepancies between emotion identification and emotion expression. It is vital to remind people that the greater the discrepancy, the greater the internal stress level. Further implications might involve...

a) headaches, stomach problems, anxiety attacks.

b) other people, due to reactions related to grief, e.g., an increase in arguments, irritability

c) confusion, frustration, and/or ambivalence

Activity

1. Explain concept of "Inside, I Feel..." / "Outside I Appear..." using the following example:

Name a situation	Inside	Outside	Implications
Anniversary of a loved one's death	(X) confused (X) miserable (X) angry (X) annoyed	(X) peaceful	ulcer feel alone and unsupported not relating to friends well

2. Distribute handouts, instructing group members to complete.

3. Ask group members to share, with emphasis on implications and ways to bridge the gap of this discrepancy.

4. Process the activity.

Variations

1. Facilitate role plays, by encouraging group members to choose situations in which they were unable to express their grief well.

   For example: *It was the anniversary of a loved one's death and I was at work. I became angry when my boss asked me to do something, so I started an argument with my co-worker.*

   Encourage group members to first do the role play as the situation actually happened, and then work on communicating their grief more effectively. Ask group members to provide support and feedback for those who are role-playing.

2. Make deck of 24 index cards using emotions listed in front of handout. Ask group members to choose a card and give an example of when they felt this way during the grief process.

Inside Outside

Name a situation in which you experience grief.	"Inside, I feel ..." (only I know that I am feeling ...)		"Outside, I appear..." (other people view me as...)		Implications of inside/outside discrepancy:
_____ _____ _____ _____ _____ _____ _____ _____ _____	☐ Aggressive ☐ Angry ☐ Annoyed ☐ Anxious ☐ Confused ☐ Depressed ☐ Disappointed ☐ Discouraged ☐ Embarrassed ☐ Exhausted ☐ Fine ☐ Guilty	☐ Helpless ☐ Hurt ☐ Lonely ☐ Miserable ☐ Peaceful ☐ Relieved ☐ Sad ☐ Shocked ☐ Sorry ☐ Undecided ☐ Withdrawn ☐ _____	☐ Aggressive ☐ Angry ☐ Annoyed ☐ Anxious ☐ Confused ☐ Depressed ☐ Disappointed ☐ Discouraged ☐ Embarrassed ☐ Exhausted ☐ Fine ☐ Guilty	☐ Helpless ☐ Hurt ☐ Lonely ☐ Miserable ☐ Peaceful ☐ Relieved ☐ Sad ☐ Shocked ☐ Sorry ☐ Undecided ☐ Withdrawn ☐ _____	☐ Physical symptoms: _____ _____ ☐ In my thoughts and feelings: _____ _____ _____ _____ ☐ In relationships: _____ _____ _____

While it *is* OK to have some discrepancies between our feelings and expressions, it is also important to recognize that the greater this discrepancy, the greater the internal stress level. Bridging the gap between inside and outside can be done in several ways. What are some of your ideas?

STEPS OF GRIEF

Leader's Guide

Submitted by Marta Felber, M.Ed.

Purpose

To become aware of stages of grief.

To identify personal stages of grief and experience feelings, past and present, at each stage.

Possible Names of Sessions

- "Denial, Shock, Anger...Sound Familiar?"
- "Where Am I in the Stages of Grief?"
- "Stages of Grief...Absolutely Normal!"

Background Information

Most people do go through stages (steps) of grief after a loss. Experiences at different stages may vary greatly, causing an individual to feel "weird", "different", and in some cases, as if s/he is "going crazy". Identifying these stages and/or feelings, sharing with others and knowing others have experienced them also, can help individuals to understand their own personal journeys through grief and feel supported in this process.

Activity

1. Review concepts as outlined in the Purpose and Background Information.

2. Ask group members to help (if appropriate), to put the names of the seven stages (steps) on the floor, using strips of ribbon or office machine tape. (Seven chairs with signs could be substituted.) If space is not available, identified lines could be drawn on a dry/erase board.

3. Instruct each person to identify his/her loss and then to locate (depending on the activity used) which stage s/he is in presently. In some groups this may be sitting on the corresponding chair, finding a place on the floor or pointing at a location on the board.

4. Distribute handouts and pencils and instruct group members to complete.

5. Share responses in a supportive atmosphere.

6. Review the "Keep in Mind" section emphasizing these important points.

Variations

1. Facilitate discussion and encourage group members to:
   a. share stages of grief that are not finished
   b. help each other with these by saying, "It was helpful for me at that stage when I _____."
   c. as a group, read aloud the *"Keep in Mind"* section.

2. Divide group into pairs. Give five minutes for each individual to share:
   a. their least comfortable stage
   b. their most comfortable stage
   c. their present stage

STEPS OF GRIEF

WE GO THROUGH [STAGES] STEPS OF GRIEF AFTER A LOSS

▶ There are many lists giving the stages of grief. One list might be:

SHOCK ▶ **SORROW** ▶ **DENIAL** ▶ **ANGER** ▶ **GUILT** ▶ **DEPRESSION** ▶ **ACCEPTANCE**

▶ Keep in mind that . . .

- Not all persons experience all of these stages after a loss.
- Stages may be repeated.
- No stage needs to last indefinitely.
- Your stages may not be in this order.
- All stages are normal.

1. Choose one of your losses and write it here: _____

_____

ACCEPTANCE

DEPRESSION

GUILT

ANGER

DENIAL

SORROW

SHOCK

2. Start with "**SHOCK**" on the stairway. Think of your loss and the feelings of shock. What did you do? Are you at this stage now? Have you already been at this stage and moved on?

Make notes on this step about your experience of being in shock.

3. Continue up the stairway, stopping on each step to "sit", think, feel, and make notes.

Healing from a Loss

Leader's Guide

Submitted by Mary Lou Hamilton, MS, RN

Purpose

To increase awareness of feelings regarding a loss and the feelings associated with the expression of healing.

To identify triggers (or stressors) that affect reactions to loss.

To identify sources of comfort in the healing process following a death or loss.

Possible Names of Sessions

- "Time for Healing"
- "Grief Work Begins Now"
- "Expressing Grief...In a Different Way"

Background Information

Each person has had an experience with loss as a source of stress. Grief and loss occur in stages. It is important to recognize and explore methods for reducing the stress associated with the feelings that occur after a loss, when healing begins to take place.

Activity

1. Introduce the topic of grief and the fact that it is universal. Explain that grief results from the pain of loss – a death, job change, disappointments, disruptions in the family, altered friendships, unfulfilled dreams or diminishing abilities.

2. Elicit examples from group members.

3. Discuss briefly the topic of imagery and relaxation to assist in grief work.

4. Distribute handouts instructing participants to fold the handout in half.

5. Place a variety of coloring supplies (paint, markers, crayons, colored pencils) in the center of the table instructing participants to select material to use for this activity. Set up an atmosphere of no talking during the art expression part of the activity. Playing soft music may assist in art expression.

6. Allow ten minutes for this part of the activity. Instruct group members to close their eyes and think of an image associated with the words "grief" or "loss" and then to open their eyes, and draw a symbol of the image on the paper. Ask group members to write words at the bottom of the page to describe the image.

7. Alow ten minutes for this part of the activity. Direct participants to close their eyes and think of the image associated with "healing" and on the second half of the paper, to draw an image of healing. Again, instruct participants to write words to describe the image at the bottom of the page (or any other words that are significant to the image drawn or painted).

8. Ask each participant to share as much as possible, forcing no one to speak if they are reluctant.

9. Ask "What are your reactions to your own art work?" Emphasize the PROCESS and not the PRODUCT, discouraging comparisons of quality differences between participants.

10. Process by exploring feelings that emerge in the expression of grief and healing (denial, depression, hope, strength, wisdom, etc.).

11. Encourage other healing and creative opportunities stemming from this grief work such as poetry, journalizing, artwork, collages, music, etc.

Variations

1. Ask participants to relax, guiding them through a deep breathing exercise for several minutes before or after the creative expression.

2. Ask group members to describe the personal patterns experienced for handling grief or loss. Are there others in the group with similar patterns? Themes? What are healthy healing hints, strategies or sources of comfort?

Healing from a Loss

Loss

Healing

GRIEF IS LIKE...

Leader's Guide
Submitted by
Libby D. Schardt, OTR/L

Purpose

To release feelings surrounding grief issues.

To use visual images of grief to assist in the healing process.

Possible Names of Sessions

• "How Do You See Your Grief?"
• "Good Grief"
• "Looking at Grief...In a New Way!"

Background Information

Grief is the process we all go through after a loss. It is also a powerful emotion and is as individual as the person experiencing it. Encouraging group members to creatively imagine how they are feeling, can help put feelings into a common language and allow for acceptance of feelings. Grieving is a process that leads to healing and personal growth.

Activity

1. Allow group members to describe their feelings of grief in their own words.

2. Explain concept of group by reviewing the background information.

3. Distribute handouts and thin markers.

4. Discuss the imagery of each picture and how it can shed light on their grief. Give or elicit an example for each picture, e.g., a wave of emotions or feelings may occur in a car when the radio is on and a certain song is playing and it reminds them of a person, place or situation.

5. Ask individuals to draw in their own images in the last two boxes and to share.

6. Ask group members to circle the images that they feel best reflects their personal grief process.

7. Process benefits of this activity.

Variations

1. After completion of activity above, ask group members to write a short story about their grief and how it feels to them, or how they perceive it to be. Ask them to include images discussed and coping skills they have used or would like to use.

2. Gather magazines and ask members to cut out pictures of what grief feels like. Create a group collage together titled "Grief looks like..." and post it for clients and families to see.

GRIEF IS LIKE...

 A Puzzle

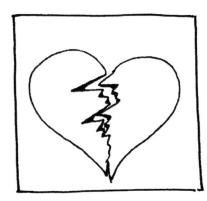 A Broken Heart

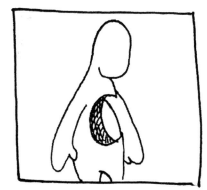 Missing Pieces or Wounds

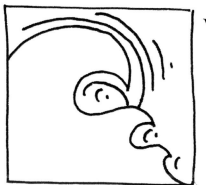 Waves

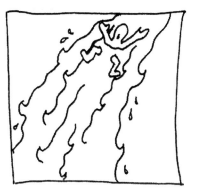 A Rapid River

 A Maze

 An Illness

 Your Drawing

 Your Drawing

Daily Record of Medicines

Leader's Guide

Purpose

To encourage the safe use of medicines by older people.

Possible Names of Sessions

- "Safety First"
- "Keeping a Good Record"
- "My Meds – My Responsibility"

Background Information

Medicine taking can be extremely complicated with the number of medication changes, long and complicated med names, and number of doctors involved, etc. Mixing up meds and taking them incorrectly can have serious implications. The activity handout is worthwhile for the older adult to complete, but also to have afterwards for personal and family reference.

Activity

1. Distribute handouts (as many as needed to each individual) and easy-to-read pens.

2. Explain background information asking for input from group members.

3. Give ten minutes for group members to complete, helping them if necessary.

4. Pair group members together to review, explaining that verbal and written review will help put it in the memory.

5. Offer realistic situations that might come up:
   a. What if the doctor changes your meds? (Offer blank handouts to group members explaining that they can photocopy the sheet in the future and make needed changes.)
   b. What should I do if I lose 'my daily record'? (Suggest that copies are made and given to loved ones for reference.)
   c. I might forget to look at my daily record … where should I put it? (Recommend a variety of places: a wallet, a medicine cabinet, the refrigerator, and elicit group input!)

6. Ask a group member to review why we did this session, and how the daily records can be a help to them for the future.

Variations

1. Use in a family meeting.

2. Ask group members to bring in all medications from home. Assist in sorting current medications from old medications.

Daily Record of Medicines

Name of Medication	Doctor who prescribed	Amount I take	Times of day I take it

Name of Medication	Doctor who prescribed	Amount I take	Times of day I take it

Name of Medication	Doctor who prescribed	Amount I take	Times of day I take it

Name of Medication	Doctor who prescribed	Amount I take	Times of day I take it

Medications And Me

Leader's Guide

Purpose

To encourage the safe use of medicines taken by older people by reviewing fundamentals of safe medication management.

Possible Names of Sessions

- "Me and My Medicines"
- "Taking 'em Right...Meds!"
- "My Body...My Responsibility!"

Background Information

Older adults may be at greater health risks as oftentimes, they take several drugs at one time. Chronic illness coupled with acute illnesses can be a complicating factor as well. Changes in the body may account for unexpected reactions from over the counter or prescribed medications.

Activity

1. List the different substances people in the group take. They may include:
   - Herbal remedies
   - Over-the-counter medicines
   - Laxatives
   - Vitamins
   - Antacids
   - Alcohol
   - Prescribed medicines for physical or emotional symptoms

2. Explain that medicine taking can be complicated and confusing.

3. Distribute handouts and pens.

4. Instruct group members to complete handout.

5. Discuss each item allowing different people to share "what might happen if someone did not do that item".

6. Problem solve obstacles that might arise if boxes are not checked off.

Variations

1. Complete handouts and allow for pair sharing to discuss which boxes are checked and for pair problem solving.

2. Bring a drug reference manual, Internet sites, and other resources to expand people's awareness of ways to find out about medicines.

Medications And Me

Drugs can be an effective health treatment for an older adult, but only when taken safely. Please check off the statements on the right if they are true almost all of the time.

❑ I take exactly the drug(s) prescribed by my doctor.

❑ I follow the dosage schedule as closely as possible.

❑ I never take anyone else's medicines other than my own.

❑ I faithfully tell my doctor(s) about past problems with medicines when s/he's considering a new one.

❑ I report any problems I'm having with medicines when I visit the doctor or before if needed.

❑ I know what the side effects of my medicines are.

❑ I can open up my medicine container(s) easily.

❑ I can read the directions clearly on all the labels.

❑ I regularly discard old medicines.

❑ I ask the pharmacist about side effects, foods or activities to avoid when I get a new prescription filled or I read the product information.

❑ I review my medicines with my doctor(s) on a regular basis.

❑ I share my DAILY RECORD OF MEDICINES with new doctors so that s/he will know what another physician is prescribing.

DEVELOPING A SYSTEM THAT WORKS

Leader's Guide

Submitted by Joan Rascati

Purpose

To increase medication management by developing healthy and supportive systems.

Possible Names of Sessions

- "My System...My Life!"
- "Organizing My Meds"
- "Time to Un-Complicate Your Meds?"

Background Information

Medication management can be a difficult task but is vital for many people to control symptoms.
Once symptoms are controlled, other functional performance areas often-times fall into place.

Activity

1. Distribute handouts and review the importance of developing a system to assist in taking medications properly.

2. Read the first section as a group and discuss the value of organizational systems. Brainstorm other creative ideas for different ways to track medications.

3. Introduce concept of *knowing who to contact* as part of a system. Instruct group members to complete section and discuss results.

4. Ask a group member to explain why an action plan would be helpful.

5. Instruct group members to complete the action plan section, offering examples as needed. Share the development of individual action plans.

6. Process by asking group members to explain why systems might be helpful and who to share the plans with, to ensure support and success.

Variations

1. Ask each individual to write on a slip of paper one concern s/he has regarding the taking of prescribed medication(s). Include the following questions, if desired, for variety and to stimulate meaningful discussions:
   a. "Will I become addicted to this medication if I stay on it for a long time?"
   b. "What should I do if I get a lot of pressure to go off of my medications?"
   c. "I can't remember when to take my medications."

   Collect the pieces of paper and answer all questions/concerns on the pieces of paper, respecting anonymity.

2. Bring a willing older adult to the group who has overcome obstacles to successfully take medications. Ask him/her to share with the group and discuss.

DEVELOPING A SYSTEM THAT WORKS *for you*

Taking medications as prescribed is vital in controlling symptoms.

DIFFERENT WAYS TO TRACK YOUR MEDICATIONS (MEDS)

Some people take several medications and this can become very complicated. Some are taken at different times with special instructions. Organizing a system will make it easier.

HERE ARE A FEW IDEAS:

1. Use a check off chart that lists what to take and when to take it. Post it near your medication supply or refrigerator.

2. Color code tops of medicine bottles with stick-on labels using same color code on a chart.

3. Store bought pillboxes are available for daily or weekly monitoring. Every morning you put the pills you need for that day in its compartment. Some may have a compartment for morning, noon, evening and bedtime. You can determine at a glance how many pills you've taken.

4. If you are having trouble remembering all of your doses, it may be possible to consolidate them. Check with your doctor.

KNOWING WHO TO CONTACT

Who should you notify ...

▶ to report side effects or problems? _____

▶ to discuss how you should deal with side effects? _____

▶ if your condition is worsening? _____

▶ if your meds become too costly? _____

▶ if stress is becoming a factor in your symptom management plan? _____

▶ if you want to adjust the dosage? _____

ACTION PLAN (TO DEVELOP A SYSTEM): _____

_____

_____

_____

_____

_____

_____

FACT SHEET

Leader's Guide

Submitted by Joan Rascati

Purpose

To increase medication management by expanding knowledge of medications and taking those medications.

Possible Names of Sessions

- "What You Need to Know About Meds"
- "Just the Facts"
- "Medications – Knowledge Applied Is Power!"

Background Information

Medication management can be a difficult task but is vital for many people in controlling symptoms. Once symptoms are controlled, other functional performance areas oftentimes fall into place. It is wise to include supportive family/friends/significant others in the medication management process.

Activity

1. Distribute handouts and pencils.

2. Review the material, encouraging brief discussion for each item covered.

3. Invite a recovering consumer to speak to the group for 20 minutes regarding his/her personal experiences with medications, trials on medications, etc.

4. Facilitate 15-minute question and answer period.

5. Add to the "Just In Case You Didn't Know" list with group input and/or with items such as...
   a. Dizziness may occur with some medications. If this is the case, change positions slowly.
   b. Each doctor needs to be aware of all medications.

6. Process the session, using the *Knowledge Applied is Power* concept.

Variations

1. Bring to the group common over-the-counter medication containers (mild pain, cold/sinus, preparations, sleep, laxatives, etc.) and information sheets from the box. Make over-sized copies on photocopier for those with impaired vision, if needed, and distribute them to group members. Ask group members to determine if they can be taken together safely, with their current medications.

2. Role-play with group members possible situations: a trip to the doctor's office; a discussion with someone urging you to go off your medications; an interaction with a supportive person dealing with the issue "But I don't want to take medications my whole life!"

FACT SHEET ▼ FACT SHEET

Everything you always wanted to know about medications…

FACTS ABOUT OVER THE COUNTER MEDICATIONS (OTC)

1. Non-prescription medications are intended to relieve symptoms of minor ailments. If conditions persist, see your doctor.

2. Some over the counter medications should NOT be taken with others. It may interfere with their effectiveness.

3. There is information on the labels that warns people who have special health problems.

4. If in doubt about purchasing an OTC medication, ask your pharmacist. This can help prevent problems.

5. Check with your pharmacist before taking any OTC medication with your prescription.

PLAYING IT SAFE…(THE NO-NO'S OR NEVER'S)

1. Never discontinue medications on your own.

2. Never take someone else's medications.

3. Never give your medication to someone else.

4. Never take the labels off your medication containers.

5. Never leave medication within the reach of children.

6. Never combine a medication from its original bottle to another.

7. Never keep prescriptions you are no longer taking.

8. Never go far from home without a list of medications.

JUST IN CASE YOU DIDN'T KNOW !!!

1. Store medications in a cool, dry place. This most likely is NOT your medicine cabinet!

2. Some medications may cause drowsiness and can make operating a car or machinery hazardous.

3. Medicine bottles may come with easy-to-open caps. Just ask your pharmacist.

4. It takes time for some medication to produce a noticeable effect.

5. Prescription medication for mental illness does not take the place of therapy or counseling.

6. It may take time for a doctor to find the right medication and dosage for you. Every person is affected differently by medications. Be patient!

NOTES: _____

_____

_____

_____

_____

DO YOU KNOW YOUR MEDS?

Leader's Guide

Submitted by Joan Rascati

Purpose

To increase medication management by expanding knowledge of medications, and taking the medications.

Possible Names of Sessions

- "Know Thy Meds"
- "Get Your Medication Questions Answered"
- "Everything You Always Wanted to Know About Your Medications"

Background Information

Medication management can be a difficult task but is vital for many people in controlling symptoms. Oftentimes, once symptoms are controlled, other functional performance areas fall into place. It is wise to include supportive significant others / family / friends in the medication management process.

Activity

1. Distribute handouts, pencils and highlighters.

2. Instruct group members to complete Section A independently.

3. Review for accuracy.

4. Encourage group members to highlight one medication for further study. Perhaps a new medication or one that a group member is unsure about. Introduce Section B by explaining that all of these questions are important to have answered, since medication management is so important in controlling symptoms.

5. Instruct group members to complete this section about the chosen medication as able and to highlight the questions that group members are unsure of, or don't have the answers.

6. Complete the highlighted items with group members, with the assistance of appropriate reference books.

7. Discuss Section C, reinforcing the importance of support with medication management.

Variations

1. Give one index card to each group member to write questions. Contribute the following questions, or others relevant to the group, to the "ASK-IT-BASKET", if needed to talk about sensitive issues:
   a. "Will this medication affect my sex life?"
   b. "Will this medication affect my weight?"
   c. "Do I have to be concerned about my exposure to sunlight when taking this medication?"
   d. "Can I drive with this medication?"
   e. "Will this medication affect my vision?"
   Answer questions or refer to staff who are knowledged in this area.

2. Stimulate and support controversy as a way of dealing with issues. Discuss openly the topic of "How to handle or live with side effects."

DO YOU KNOW YOUR MEDS?

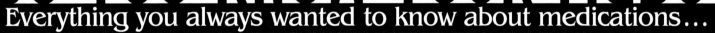

Everything you always wanted to know about medications…

A. WHAT MEDICATIONS DO YOU TAKE NOW?

_____   _____

_____   _____

_____   _____

_____   _____

B. CAN YOU ANSWER EACH OF THESE QUESTIONS ABOUT YOUR MEDS?

1. The name of one of my meds is… _____

2. How does this medication help me? _____

3. What is the medication for? _____

4. What kind of medication is it? _____

5. How often should I take it? _____

6. How long should I take it? _____

7. How should I take it? (before or after meals, with water, etc.)

_____

8. What times of the day should I take it? _____

9. What are the side effects? _____

10. What can I do to reduce the side effects? _____

11. How does it mix with other medications? _____

12. Are there certain foods to avoid? _____

13. Do I need a blood test? _____

14. Is the medication addictive? _____

15. Does it mix with alcohol? _____

16. What should I do if I miss a dose? _____

17. How will this medication affect my lifestyle? _____

When you are prescribed medication, the questions to the left and above are the ones to ask!

C. If you didn't have all of the answers about your meds, where can you go to find the answers? _____

_____

Who can or should you share this information with? _____

_____

Crossword Puzzle

Leader's Guide

Purpose

To increase awareness of commonly used terms in mental health and aging programs.

Possible Names of Sessions

- "Crossword Puzzle with a Mission"
- "Oh, I Get It!"
- "Do You Have a Clue?"

Background Information

Terms are often used without everyone's understanding. Some people are shy or embarrassed and don't ask for explanation while others may misunderstand terms. A review of the meanings of commonly used terms in a fun, nonthreatening way will literally 'put everyone on the same page'.

Hyphenated words have no hyphen or space between. Two-word phrase has no space between it.

Activity

1. Distribute handouts and easy-to-read pens.

2. Review purpose of this crossword puzzle.

3. Divide group in pairs or allow group members to do individually, depending on skill level and interest.

4. Give group ten to fifteen minutes to complete.

5. Review answers and allow group members to discuss terms. Provide information not included in Clues.

6. Ask group members to make an additional list of commonly heard terms by professionals or in the literature.

Variations

1. Develop a word search of terms listed in Activity #6.

2. Tally group members to see which of the terms need further exploration.

Answers to Clues

Across

2. therapist

4. forgiveness

6. OTC

7. isolated

8. brain

11. anxious

12. depression

Down

1. self-medicate

3. supports

5. mental illness

9. aging

10. legacy

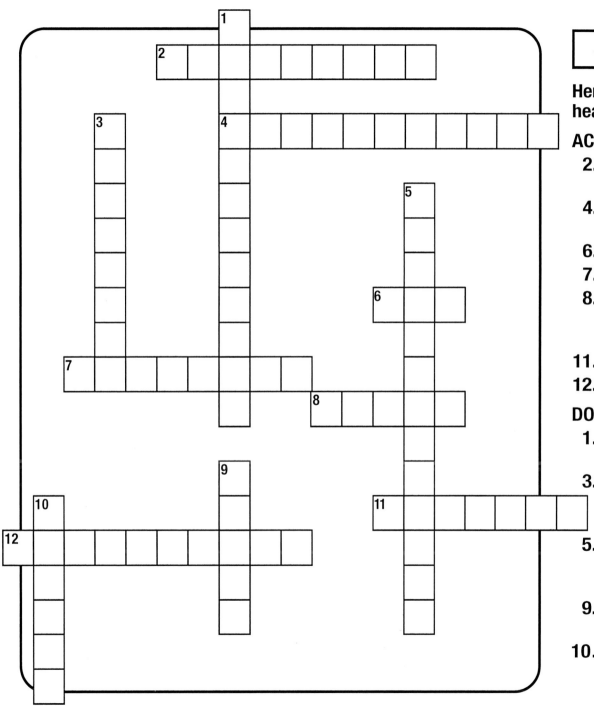

Crossword Puzzle

Here are clues to some aging and /or mental health terms.

ACROSS

2. A professional who listens and works towards mental wellness

4. A theme that might appear in an older adult's life that needs resolve

6. Over the counter drugs abbreviation

7. Feeling separated from others

8. What needs to be exercised in older adulthood? Sometimes associated with the common expression "use it or lose it"

11. Nervous, tense, high-strung

12. Persistent sadness over time

DOWN

1. What some people do to relieve symptoms; not a recommended course of action

3. Those people or agencies who help and care about you and advocate for your best interest

5. A term that includes a variety of disorders including anxiety disorders, depression, personality disorders, etc.

9. The natural process that begins the moment we are born

10. What we will leave for generations to come

Move Away From the Myths

Leader's Guide

Purpose

To increase awareness of aging and depression.

Possible Names of Sessions

- "Keeping Up-To-Date"
- "TRUE or FALSE – Depression and Older Adults"
- "Depression – Is It Significant in Older Adults?"

Background Information

Many older adults have fears about depression and mental illness and recognize myths as truths. The reality is that depression is treatable. It is often under recognized and overlooked. It is time to educate older adults and their loved ones about the realities of this subject for prevention and treatment.

Activity

1. Ask group members what is the first thing they think of when they think of the word "psychiatry". Write all words on a flipchart in large print.

2. Ask group members if some of these thoughts might have prevented them from either getting help or getting a loved one help.

3. Distribute handouts and easy-to-read pens.

4. Give group members ten minutes to circle the correct response.

5. Discuss responses. Dispel myths with answers.

1. True	6. False
2. True	7. True
3. True	8. False
4. False	9. True
5. False	10. True

6. Ask group members to share this paper with loved ones.

Variations

1. Cut myths into strips and give one to each group member, one by one. Ask them to read it aloud and guess the answer. Then give the correct answer and discuss.

2. Arrange to have an older adult who is in recovery from depression come and speak to the group about his/her experiences.

Move Away From the Myths

Understanding Older Adults and Depression

Our culture holds myths about older adults and health issues. Take this TRUE and FALSE QUIZ and see how much you really know about older adults and depression. Circle either TRUE or FALSE.

		TRUE	FALSE
1.	Older adults often deny a depression.	TRUE	FALSE
2.	Memory complaints and bodily complaints are signs of a depression.	TRUE	FALSE
3.	Hearing loss may be a contributing factor to depression in an older adult.	TRUE	FALSE
4.	A depressed mood is the same thing as a clinical depression.	TRUE	FALSE
5.	Depression does not frequently occur with other medical illnesses.	TRUE	FALSE
6.	Depression is not a significant predictor of suicide in older adults.	TRUE	FALSE
7.	A first depression of an older adult may be his or her last.	TRUE	FALSE
8.	Depression is a normal part of aging.	TRUE	FALSE
9.	Changes in sleeping habits and appetite are signs of depression.	TRUE	FALSE
10.	Suicide rates in late life are higher than any other point in the life course.	TRUE	FALSE

It is important to be educated about the realities of this important subject. Share this handout with your loved ones.

I'll Never Forget the Day I ...

Leader's Guide

Purpose

To reminisce, tell stories, and listen to promote healthy aging.

Possible Names of Sessions

- "The Good Ole Days!"
- "Do You Remember?"
- "Storytelling for All"

Background Information

Recalling memories is a healthy part of aging. It is a normal activity and helps validate the older adult by having others listen to their memorable life experiences. Storytelling can be touching, moving and of great value to the storyteller and to the listener. Listening to others can help us feel connected, alive and filled with emotions. This activity should be success-oriented and adapted so that it will be just that.

Activity

1. Arrange chairs in a circle.

2. Explain the importance of being able to remember and being a good listener.

3. Distribute the handouts.

4. Ask the person on your left to begin with number one. S/he will choose from the first or second prompt and tell a story.

5. Proceed around the circle allowing all group members to successfully tell at least one story.

6. Develop a new list of prompts that weren't included in this list for another session!

Variations

1. Use as a part of an intergenerational activity.

2. Allow other members of the group to share a story about the second prompt that did not get chosen.

I'll Never Forget the Day I ...

1. **got kissed for the first time**   or   **drove a car for the first time by myself**

2. **heard about the tooth fairy (or Santa Claus)** or   **got a new pet**

3. **experienced someone close to me dying**   or   **heard really bad news**

4. **got in really big trouble by my parents**   or   **really got in trouble in school**

5. **got my first job**   or   **could afford** _____

6. **told a lie and got caught**   or   **disappointed my** _____

7. **tried something I shouldn't have**   or   **really got hurt**

8. **got married**   or   **experienced the miracle of** _____

9. **traveled to** _____   or   **had a child**

10. **met my in-laws**   or   **got my first raise**

11. **got drunk for the first time**   or   **got sick away from home**

12. **realized I was a grown up**   or   **bought my first house**

13. **did something I knew was really stupid**   or   **I got a really bad grade in school**

14. **got caught doing something**   or   **really embarrassed myself**

15. **rode a bike for the first time**   or   **played an important game**

Sing, Sing A Song

Leader's Guide

Submitted by
Sylvia T. Schwartzman, RN, MS

Purpose

To recall old song titles and tap into memories of bygone times and share experiences with one another.

Possible Names of Sessions

- "Hum a Few Bars!"
- "Memory and Music"
- "Oh Yeah, That's It!"

Background Information

This fun activity for older adults can be used as a reminiscence and recall activity. Music oftentimes holds fond memories of the song itself and the surrounding times and circumstances.

Activity

1. Distribute handouts and easy to read pens.

2. Play as individuals or in teams by asking group members to fill in the blanks to the best of their abilities.

3. Share responses.

4. Generate discussions of who sang the song, what was happening in their lives when this song was popular and if they have other memories associated with the songs.

Key

My **Blue** Heaven

Pennsylvania **6500**

Over the **Rainbow**

Chattanooga Choo, Choo

Don't Sit Under the **Apple** Tree

That Old Black **Magic**

Dancing **Cheek** to **Cheek**

Loving that **Man** of Mine

Me and My **Shadow**

America, the Beautiful

Oh, Danny **Boy**

I Left My Heart in **San Francisco**

Sidewalks of **New York**

Star Dust

Little **Brown** Jug

I Dream of **Jeannie** with the Light Brown Hair

Nothing Could be **Finer** than to be in **Carolina** in the Morning

Sweet **Adeline**, My Adeline

Someone's in the Kitchen with **Dinah**

You Are My **Sunshine**, My Only **Sunshine**

Dancing in the Dark

Mares Eat Oats and **Does** Eat Oats and **Little Lambs** Eat Ivy

When the **Saints** Go Marching In

Sentimental **Journey**

You Made Me **Love** You

As **Time** Goes By

Variations

1. Bring in an audiotape of these songs and play them after clients have identified each one.

2. Encourage a sing-a-long by having words to each song printed out in large print for people to follow along.

Sing, Sing A Song

Fill in the blanks of these song titles:

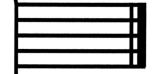

My _____ Heaven

Pennsylvania _____

Over the _____

_____ Choo, Choo

Don't Sit Under the _____ Tree

That Old Black _____

Dancing _____ to _____

Loving that _____ of Mine

Me and My _____

_____, the Beautiful

Oh, Danny _____

I Left My Heart in

_____ _____

Sidewalks of _____ _____

_____ Dust

Little _____ Jug

I Dream of _____

   with the Light Brown Hair

Nothing Could Be _____ than to Be

in _____ in the Morning

Sweet _____, My _____

Someone's in the Kitchen with _____

You Are My _____,

  My Only _____

_____ In the Dark

_____ Eat Oats and _____

Eat Oats and _____

_____ Eat Ivy

When the _____ Go Marching In

Sentimental _____

You Made Me _____ You

As _____ Goes By

The Floor Plan

Leader's Guide

Purpose

To share positive memories and stories of the past using a floor plan and objects of the past as cues and memory stimulators.

Possible Names of Sessions

- "Bringing Up Some Favorite Memories"
- "Recalling the Good Times"
- "Who'd a Thought?"

Background Information

Wouldn't we love to get a glimpse of our childhood or early years one more time? For those of us with a mostly positive past, the answer would be "yes". For those people who have experienced trauma and have mostly negative feelings of the past, the answer would be "no!" and this activity would not be advised for them. For many, using stimulating prompts such as visually looking at floor plans and "actively" seeking for objects might prove to be exciting, challenging and fun!

Activity

1. Screen participants for appropriateness of activity.

2. Describe activity briefly to particpants.

3. Distribute handouts and easy-to read pens or markers.

4. Give group ten to fifteen minutes to complete.

5. Offer rulers if participants need them for creating new or additional rooms.

6. Play soothing music in the background.

7. When completed, ask participants to share a story that came up for them during the activity.

8. After sharing, discuss commonalities of age (range) participants were when they remembered, objects and stories.

Variations

1. Bring in objects that were treasures or memories for you and have others do the same to share in the next session.

2. As a follow-up activity, create a collage from the entire group titled "We Remember!" looking for objects remembered in magazines, catalogues, or any other printed material.

The Floor Plan

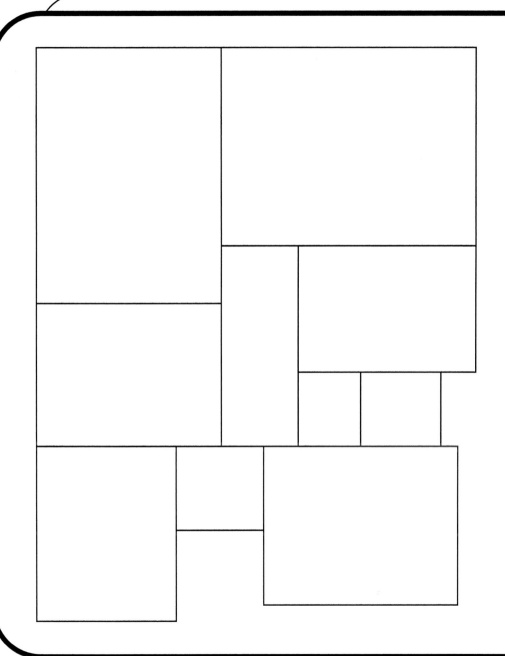

It is possible to remember certain things from our past with simple cues. Think of your earliest memories of a house.

Here's a sample floor plan of a home. If this works for you, then use it. If you need to adapt it, then move lines or rooms around, or draw your own on the back of this sheet.

1. Label the rooms: living room, kitchen, dining room, bathroom, bedroom, etc.

2. Identify one interesting object in each room: kitchen (curtains), bedroom (jewelry box).

3. Think of an interesting, positive story about one or more of the rooms or any of the objects.

When Was the Last Time I Heard That?

Leader's Guide

Purpose

To use sayings as a means of reminiscence, story-telling and values discussions.

Possible Names of Sessions

- "My Mom/Dad Said That!"
- "The Sages Speak!"
- "Words to the Wise"

Background Information

There might be a lot of wisdom in old sayings. There are also a lot of memories attached to them as they taught values during the growing years. They are short and usually easy to remember and lend themselves well to discussions.

Activity

1. Write on the board: *Don't Cry Over Spilt Milk*.

2. Ask group members to explain what this means.

3. Explain that these sayings are often values-based and were often told to us when we "needed to hear them." Ask the group if anyone really remembers hearing that expression…especially when they were growing up. Invite them to share the story.

4. Distribute handouts and highlighters.

5. Ask group members to highlight two to four of their favorite sayings, especially if they can remember it from the past.

6. Ask everyone to contribute by referring them to the directions at the bottom of the page.

7. Offer opportunities to share.

Variations

1. Develop a new list of sayings and expressions that were not listed on this activity sheet.

2. Play a guessing letter game with the sayings. For example: _ *(A watched pot never boils)*

When Was the Last Time I Heard That?

Remember these sayings you heard when you were younger?

A stitch in time saves nine

You can catch more flies with honey than vinegar

A penny saved is a penny earned

A bird in the hand is worth two in the bush

Waste not want not

Count your blessings

Never put off till tomorrow what you can do today

Buyer beware

Sink or swim

Here today, gone tomorrow

Respect your elders

You can't take it with you

Children should be seen and not heard

Birds of a feather flock together

Act your age!

Look before you leap

You are what you eat

Don't speak ill of the dead

Laughter is the best medicine

Do unto others as you would have others do unto you

1. Recall what one of the sayings means.
2. Recall a time when you heard it.
3. Decide if that saying still has meaning in your life.
4. Is there another saying that had a special meaning to you when you were younger that is not on this page?

EMERGENCY INFORMATION

Leader's Guide

Submitted by
Melissa L. Oliver, OTR/L, MS
Vicki L. Addison, COTA

Purpose

To improve safety by making important emergency information easily accessible.

Possible Names of Sessions

- "Safe and Sound"
- "Cue Card for Safety"
- "Who Can Help?"

Background Information

Emergency situations generally cause confusion. Therefore important emergency information located in strategic places can assist an individual during the stressful situation. This cue card increases the probability of being able to access help, stay safe in the home and can possibly save lives.

Activity

1. Introduce and explain purpose of the emergency cue card.

2. Ask each individual to complete, using telephone books if necessary.

3. Ask individuals what other information that they would like to see on this card.

4. Encourage them to write it in.

5. Photocopy as many as they need (number of phones they have) on colored paper/card stock.

6. Role play emergency and non-emergency situations with emergency information sheet and telephone.

Variations

1. Use with a client who is being discharged from a facility along with his / her family members.

2. Ask individuals what concerns they have regarding safety in their homes.

Special Note

If 9-1-1 is not used where you live, use correctional liquid paper and write in appropriate emergency number.

EMERGENCY INFORMATION

Place this information by all telephones!

911 = EMERGENCY ((fire, police, ambulance))

YOUR Address:

YOUR Phone Number:

EMERGENCY Contact Person

Name:

Phone Number:

DOCTOR'S Name:

DOCTOR'S Number:

Other:

KITCHEN SAFETY

Leader's Guide

Submitted by Melissa L. Oliver, OTR/L, MS
and Vicki L. Addison, COTA

Purpose

To increase safety in the kitchen by using a visual cue card.

Possible Names of Sessions

- "Kitchen Safety Reminders"
- "Kitchen Cues"
- "Better Safe Than Sorry!"

Background Information

Visual reminders assist with providing a safe environment for individuals who require memory aides. Kitchens are a frequent place for slips, burns, cuts and accidental fires.

Activity

1. Take participating individuals to kitchen area.

2. Introduce and explain purpose of checklist.

3. Distribute handouts and pens for notes.

4. Discuss each item on the checklist and the relevance of each item.

5. Ask group members to add anything necessary at the bottom of the list.

6. Practice completing the checklist.

7. Explore possible locations to hang the checklist at home.

8. Recommend using the checklist daily when it is first placed in the home.

9. Replace checklist weekly or laminate the checklist and use dry erase markers.

Variations

1. Demonstrate helpful kitchen equipment that might promote safety (e.g., kitchen timer, mitts, one-handed adaptive tools, fire extinguisher).

2. Demonstrate or show pictures of injury-prone areas in the kitchen, e.g., floor rugs, frayed cords, telephone lines on floor, towels by the stove. Discuss how to prevent accidents or injuries in the kitchen.

K I T C H E N   S A F E T Y

CHECK THE FOLLOWING ITEMS:

	SUNDAY	MONDAY	TUESDAY	WEDNESDAY	THURSDAY	FRIDAY	SATURDAY
Turn handles in toward the back of the stove							
Don't put knives in dish water							
Place cooking items on lower shelves							
Clean kitchen after each meal							
Turn stove / oven off after cooking							
Have chair available if you become tired							
Use available adaptive tools, gadgets or equipment to insure safety							
Turn appliances off after using							
Other: _____							
Other: _____							
Other: _____							

SAFE AND SOUND...

Leader's Guide

Purpose

To promote safety in older adults.

Possible Names of Sessions

- "Safety First"
- "Preventing Accidents at Home...Today!"
- "Is Your Home Safe for You?"

Background Information

Falls and fires are potential safety hazards with the older adult population. Adapting the environment may require a little thought, time and money but could prevent a serious accident and keep someone at home...safe and sound!

Activity

1. Distribute handouts and easy-to-read pens.

2. Use the graphics as a conversation starter of potential hazards.

3. Give group members ten minutes to complete handouts emphasizing honesty.

4. Discuss each item. Problem solve ways to increase safety when there are 'no's'.

5. Bring adapted equipment, lighting and other household equipment catalogues (with fire extinguisher, non-slip pads, lighting) to review availability and costs of needed products. Review and discuss.

6. Explain that the costs spent on preventing an accident would be substantially less than if an accident actually occurred.

Variations

1. Bring adaptive equipment to group session and demonstrate its usefulness. Display an attitude of, "You might not need this today, but please consider that someday this might be helpful."

2. Before group session, show either hand-drawn pictures or cutouts from magazines of potential hazards (wet floors, dangling or frayed cords, unsafe electrical outlets, etc.) in the home and discuss.

SAFE AND SOUND...
looking to avoid potential safety problems

Answer these questions honestly about your current living situation (if someone were to walk in your home right now).

1. Do you have loose floor rugs secured with non-slip mats under them?

2. Are all pieces of furniture sturdy with no wobbles?

3. If needed, do you have adapted equipment (grab bars, raised toilet seat, etc.) in the bathroom?

4. Do you have a list of easy-to-read emergency phone numbers with doctor's names, family members, the fire department or medical centers close to the phone?

5. Do you have properly working smoke detectors?

6. Do you have a fire extinguisher in the kitchen?

7. When you are home, do you always wear sensible, comfortable shoes?

8. Are tight spots and stairways clutter-free?

9. Do you have adequate lighting for walking at night?

10. Are commonly used items in the bathroom and kitchen reachable without a step stool?

YES   NO

Consider that any 'no's may indicate you need to adapt your environment to prevent an accident or injury.

SAFETY FIRST

Leader's Guide
Submitted by Libby D. Schardt, OTR/L

Purpose

To increase safety awareness by evaluating answers to basic home safety questions.

To help determine level of independence and level of supervision needed to remain safe.

Possible Names of Sessions

- "Wanting You to Be Safe!"
- "Safety is A Serious Matter"
- "What to Do to Keep Safe?"

Background Information

Safety is a major concern of everyone involved with older adults. Fires, falls and flus are just a few concerns! Answering questions of safety will serve as a screening to help determine how safe an individual is and how much assistance might be needed. Further assessment would be needed if red flags of unsafe behavior were detected. Answers to questions can also be used to gain information about cognitive functioning skills such as problem solving, decision-making, memory, reality orientation and judgment. Insight can also be observed.

Activity

1. Distribute handouts and easy-to-read pens.

2. Ask group members to complete handout or discuss each question and answer.

3. As a group, discuss all responses and facilitate feedback from group members. NOTE: Not all questions may be appropriate for all participants. Use discretion and ask for clarification whenever a group member's answers are unclear.

4. Process benefits of safety in the home and the risks of not being safe.

Variations

1. Ask group members to write on index cards a 'safety scenario'. For example, "You are home alone and you hear noises outside by your window. What is the best thing to do?" Switch index cards with a partner. Have group members read each other's questions and respond. Reconvene as a large group and share results of the exercise.

2. Create additional questions or use these:
   a. What should you do if there's a tornado warning?
   b. How can you tell when chicken is thoroughly cooked?
   c. Who should you call if you lose power or water in your home?
   d. Who would you call if you need a ride to an appointment?
   e. When should you lock your doors?

SAFETY FIRST · SAFETY FIRST · SAFETY FIRST
SAFETY FIRST · SAFETY FIRST · SAFETY FIRST

Here's a checklist of questions that test your safety awareness.

1. What should you do if you are having chest pains? _____

2. When washing dishes, how do you get the water the right temperature? _____

3. How do you get something off a high shelf? _____

4. Who should you call if you have severe flu symptoms? _____

   Do you know the telephone number?   Yes / No   If yes, what is it? _____

   If not, where would you find the phone number? _____

5. How often should you check the smoke detectors? _____

6. What should you wear if you're going to be outside for 10 minutes or more and it's below 32 degrees?

   _____

7. What do you do if you smell gas in your home? _____

8. Do you have a cord running across the middle of any of your floors? What might be a problem with that?

   _____

9. Is it ever OK for you or anyone else to smoke in bed? Why or why not? _____

10. Why are bathmats in the bathroom a good idea? _____

THINGS TO DO BEFORE GOING TO BED

Leader's Guide

Submitted by
Vicki L. Addison, COTA
and Melissa L. Oliver, MS, OTR/L

Purpose

To provide a checklist to assist in developing a safe and productive nightly routine.

Possible Names of Sessions

- "Sleeping Safe and Sound"
- "What Do I Need To Do?"
- "My Nightly Routine"

Background Information

Visual reminders such as checklists can provide a safer environment for those who require visual cuing. This handout can assist with initiating and completing nightly routines.

Activity

1. Introduce and explain purpose for checklist. Explain that there are several reasons people might benefit from checklists; sometimes memory or attention is poor due to depression, trauma, preoccupations with thoughts or symptoms of another illness.

2. Distribute handouts, pens and highlighters.

3. Give group members time to review columns on the left and to highlight only those that they will complete (e.g., a person who doesn't want to be awoken by an alarm clock wouldn't highlight 'alarm clock is set').

4. Then, discuss each item and the importance related to good health and safety.

5. Give group members time to add to the list, e.g., read, drink warm milk, give thanks.

6. Explore possible locations for the checklist to be hung at home.

7. Recommend daily contact from the time the checklist is first placed at home until a routine is developed or its continued use to maintain safety.

Variations

1. Replace checklist weekly or laminate the checklist and use dry erase markers.

2. Use this checklist as part of a treatment plan.

THINGS TO DO BEFORE GOING TO BED

CHECK THE FOLLOWING ITEMS:	SUNDAY	MONDAY	TUESDAY	WEDNESDAY	THURSDAY	FRIDAY	SATURDAY
Bath or shower							
Wash face							
Put on night clothes							
Brush teeth/clean dentures							
Take medicine							
Go to the bathroom							
Wash hands							
MAKE SURE THAT THE...							
Lights are turned off in bedroom							
Lights are turned off in living room							
Lights are turned off in bathroom							
Lights are turned off in kitchen							
Oven is off							
Iron is off							
Small kitchen appliances are off							
TV is off							
Radio is off							
Things are off the floor							
Doors are locked							
Windows are locked							
Alarm clock is set							
Night light is on							
Other: _____							
Other: _____							
Other: _____							
Other: _____							

Celebrate YOU!

Leader's Guide
Submitted by Sandra Christensen, BA

Purpose

To focus on special attributes of an individual.

To appreciate one's own uniqueness.

Possible Names of Sessions

• "Strength Building"
• "Time to BRAG!"
• "Why Not Tell It Like It Is!"

Background Information

Many of us are very self-critical; we have an easier time talking about our faults, limitations and deficits than our strengths, talents and qualities. This exercise is designed to give participants permission to celebrate their positive attributes.

Activity

1. Tell participants that you are giving them permission to brag!

2. Distribute handouts and easy-to-read pens.

3. Ask each person to complete the sentences with examples of ways they are growing and changing, and things that they like about their bodies, minds and spirits.

4. Ask participants to share at least one of their statements with the rest of the group. If the group is large, you may wish to divide the group into smaller groups. Four is an ideal number. No one should be pressured to share a response.

5. When participants share their responses, ask them to stand up and read the statement in a convincing way – to "say it like you mean it".

6. Suggest that participants put these statements in a place where they will see them and read them on a daily basis. The boxes can even be cut apart and put in a variety of places- taped to a bathroom mirror, the dashboard of a car or inside a calendar/daily planner.

Variations

1. Discuss how media, both TV and print, has a role in how we see ourselves. Bring examples of over-idealized men and women in pictures, headlines and captions via video clips, commercials, catalogue ads, covers of magazines, etc.

2. After giving participants a few minutes to write responses, ask them to share their answers to the first statement by going around the group and having each person read his or her response aloud. Allow individuals to 'pass' if they choose, but the 'penalty' for passing is that you must listen to compliments from other group members. For example, if a person does not share what she likes about her spirit, the other group members will tell her something positive they appreciate about her spirit.

Celebrate YOU!

Many of us are more comfortable discussing our faults than we are affirming our strengths. If you want to feel good about yourself and who you are, it's important to give yourself permission to brag a little – to celebrate the unique, loving, capable person that is YOU!

Complete each sentence below with the first response that comes to your mind.

! One of the ways that I am learning and growing is... _____

_____

! One of the positive changes I've made in my life is... _____

_____

! One of the things I like about my body is... _____

_____

! One of the things I like about my mind is... _____

_____

! One of the things I like about my spirit is... _____

_____

GOOD FOR ME!

Leader's Guide

Submitted by Judith A. Lutz, BA

Purpose

To improve self-awareness and self-esteem, by acknowledging strengths and achievements.

Possible Names of Sessions

- "Self Talk is Positive Talk"
- "Can I See the Good in EVERYTHING?"
- "Tooting My Own Horn!"

Background Information

People oftentimes get in the habit of focusing only on limitations or problems. This exercise forces one to identify strengths and engage in self-appreciation.

Activity

1. Distribute handouts and easy-to-read pens.

2. Review as a group. Then give group members time to complete individually.

3. Ask group members to find at least one statement they are comfortable reading aloud.

4. Discuss comfort level or discomfort level that group members have in identifying positives about themselves.

5. Challenge group members to acknowledge truthfulness of statements and worthiness of themselves to receive thanks.

Variations

1. Cut each open-ended statement into strips. Put in basket and have group members draw strips of paper and verbally complete. Encourage group to give feedback to individuals making statements, possibly through applause or affirming statements such as "That must have been tough" or "That's worth remembering".

2. Pursue discussion of how difficult this exercise is for young vs. older people. Are there any special challenges facing older adults when doing this type of exercise?

GOOD FOR ME!

What have you done for yourself lately? Make a list.

Note to self:

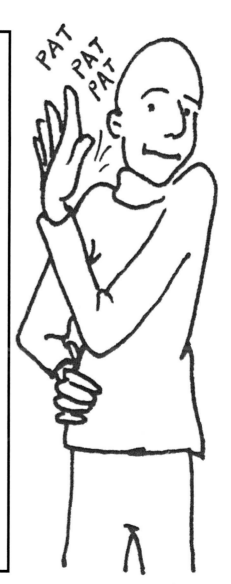

Thanks for trying _____

Thanks for saying _____

Thanks for achieving the goal of _____

Thanks for being patient when _____

Thanks for forgiving me when _____

Thanks for keeping _____

Thanks for remembering _____

Thanks for learning _____

Thanks for the natural talent of _____

Thanks for allowing _____

How Does Your Garden Grow?

Leader's Guide

Submitted by
Kimberly D. Heath, MA

Purpose

To focus on the positive qualities and work toward maintaining a positive outlook.

Possible Names of Sessions

- "Tending the Garden"
- "Nurture the Positive"
- "Flower Power"

Background Information

Negative thoughts are powerful and pervasive and they can "choke out" positive thoughts. Writing down persistent negative thoughts increases awareness of them and can lead to more rapid thought stopping. This, in turn, can lead to the ability to change negative thoughts into positive thoughts.

Activity

1. Introduce topic by reviewing background information.

2. Distribute handouts and easy-to-read pens.

3. Ask each group member to think about the negative thoughts they routinely say to themselves. Ask them to write these thoughts on the left in the "weeds" column. Offer examples: "I can't do this." "No one cares about me." "I'm not good enough."

4. Ask group members to think about any positive thoughts they routinely say to themselves. Ask them to write these thoughts on the right in the "plants" column. Offer examples: "I have friends and family who can help me." "I've done tougher things than this before." "I have faith."

5. Ask the group members to identify the most prominent negative and positive thought at the bottom of the page and to share.

6. Process by formulating individual plans to maintain positive thoughts or having a "weed-free garden".

Variations

1. Give small plants as a symbolic, token gift upon completion of session or program.

2. Discuss the impacts negative thinking has on self-esteem, health, relationships and energy level. Demonstrate this through skits generated by group members.

How Does Your Garden Grow?

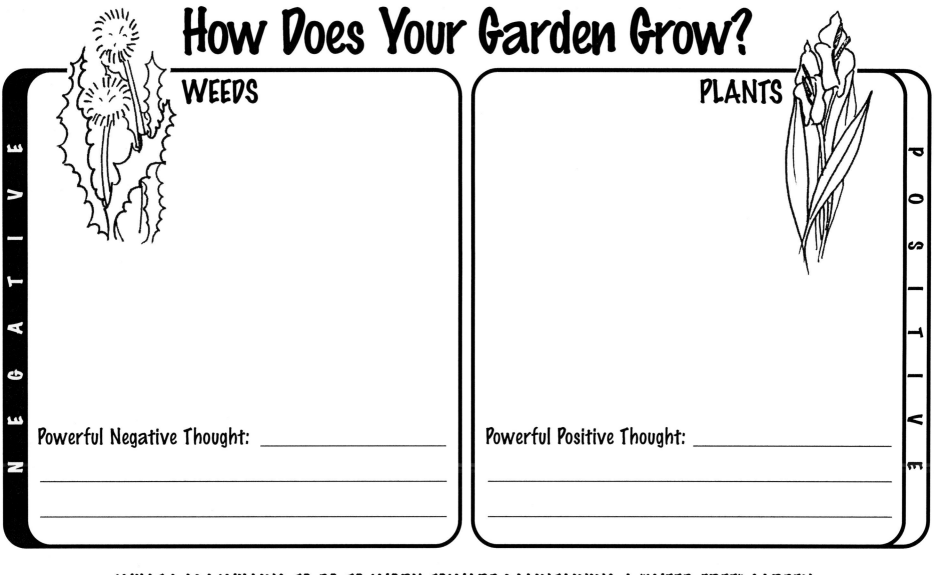

WEEDS

PLANTS

NEGATIVE

POSITIVE

Powerful Negative Thought: _____

_____

_____

Powerful Positive Thought: _____

_____

_____

WHAT I AM WILLING TO DO TO WORK TOWARD MAINTAINING A "WEED-FREE" GARDEN:

_____

_____

_____

HOW I GREW TO BE WHO I AM

Leader's Guide

Purpose

To do a life review activity with a universal metaphor of a tree to enhance self-awareness and self-esteem.

Possible Names of Sessions

- "My Life In a Nutshell...or Tree"
- "Where Did I Come From...
   Where Am I Now"
- "Do You Know What's Happening?"

Background Information

The theme of using a tree in artwork and therapy is well explored and its universal nature remains appealing. This simple activity explores people's beginnings, their development and who they are today. Life reviews can enhance self-awareness and self-esteem and be life affirming.

Activity

1. Prepare a flipchart or dry/erase board with a similar tree as the one seen in the handout. Write on the flipchart "LIFE IS LIKE A TREE".

2. Ask group members what the roots might symbolize and write all responses by the bottom of the tree. Accept all answers. Then, ask what the bark might symbolize and write all responses. Lastly, ask group members what the top branches or fruit might symbolize and write all responses.

3. Distribute handouts and easy-to-read pens.

4. Discuss group responses and compare with concepts on the handout.

5. Give group members ten to fifteen minutes to complete.

6. Divide group into pairs for five to ten minutes to share responses.

7. Reconvene and ask group members what the most interesting insight they gained from doing this exercise.

Variations

1. Develop additional questions for each section that were not on the handout and discuss.

2. Allow seniors to share this work with those who are interested (e.g., volunteers, family members, neighbors).

HOW I GREW TO BE WHO I AM

The fruits of my labor (the later years):

I am proud of my ability to _____.

I am proud that I have created or helped to create

_____.

I am proud that I stand for _____.

Today, I am known for _____.

The growth and development (the middle years):

I overcame _____,

and learned _____.

Back then, I was known as _____.

My roots (the early years):

My cultural heritage is _____.

The people who raised me are _____.

Values I was taught as a youngster were _____.

Seeing My Strengths...
That's Who I Am

Leader's Guide

Purpose

To recognize strengths as an important part of self-advocacy, to be an active member of the healthcare team and increase self-esteem.

Possible Names of Sessions

- "Strengths R US"
- "Digging For Gold"
- "Using Our Strength For Good!"

Background Information

The healthcare system documents and gets reimbursed by looking at deficits and problems. Unfortunately, people oftentimes get looked at in that way as well. By looking at strengths, we encourage the older adults to see themselves as able rather than dis-abled, having resources and being able to make good choices. As healthcare professionals we can refer to these strengths in conversations with the senior, with family members and friends, and with professional staff. We can also note these in documentation.

Activity

1. Distribute handout and easy-to-read pens.

2. Explain basic concept recognizing that there are always obstacles in our paths. The strengths help us get around the obstacles.

3. Give group members ten minutes to complete, clarifying as needed.

4. Divide group into triads and give them ten to fifteen minutes to share.

5. Reconvene and ask group members to share what was learned.

6. Ask:
   a. How can knowing your strengths be helpful to you? To your healthcare team?

   b. Why is talking about strengths difficult for some people?

   c. How did it feel to talk about strengths, resources, and assets rather than deficits, inabilities and losses?

Variations

1. Ask group members to share this handout with one significant other asking for feedback. Share results at next meeting.

2. Introduce group by writing *If we only focus on our deficits and losses, then ...* and ask group members to complete the sentence.

Seeing My Strengths ... That's Who I Am

It's an easy trap to fall into...only looking at problems, illness, disability and losses.
What might happen if we looked at positives: strengths, assets, and what we have rather than
what we don't have? In which of the following categories do you have at least one strength?

skills	interests	life experiences	financial resources
family	physical body	community support	cultural background
knowledge	spirit	emotional health	...or any other
friends	relationships	strengths!	categories you find

Write the name of the category on the line in a box.
Then, write in the boxes any assets or strengths you have in that category.

© 2003 Wellness Reproductions & Publishing   1.800.669.9208

What Do I Have To Offer?

Leader's Guide

Purpose

To find or create meaning through 'sharing'.

Possible Names of Sessions

- "Sharing is Caring"
- "Do You Dare to Share?"
- "The Greatest Gift---Yourself!"

Background Information

Older adults sometimes feel that they have little or nothing to share. They may feel useless, worthless and overlooked. It is important to be aware that older adults have more life experience, more knowledge in certain areas and oftentimes more time to give. Problem solving ways to share might be a method to get the ball rolling.

Activity

1. Write on the board "HAVING WORTH".

2. Ask group members to discuss the meaning of this phrase and list responses on the board.

3. Discuss that throughout our lifetimes, we all have worth. One way to look at that is to consider what each of us has to offer.

4. Distribute handouts and easy-to-read pens.

5. Give group members ten minutes to complete. Offer real-life examples to assist in finding ideas. E.g., **2. SHARE A SKILL** may include: being on a committee, teaching young people how to play Mah Jongg, poker, euchre, giving a talk at the library on a topic others might find interesting, etc. Keep examples down-to-earth so that people can easily relate.

6. Share responses and develop plans how to turn talk into action.

Variations

1. Bring in a local senior who shares in an interesting way and ask him/her to tell how s/he got started and the personal benefits.

2. Ask group members to discuss if any older person had ever shared anything they still treasure (not material objects).

What Do I Have To Offer?

Remember the adage, 'It's nice to share?' That's still true! Older adults have valuable experiences, skills and knowledge. As we get older, it is important to continue to share. We feel our own value and help the next generation at the same time! Here are a few ideas to increase your sharing…

1. Be a role model. See yourself as someone people look up to. Practice behaviors that you would want to see continuing in the next generation. Which of these values can you role model?   To who?

❑ Charity _____

❑ Physically active _____

❑ Healthy eating _____

❑ Continually learning _____

❑ Reading _____

❑ Having fun _____

❑ Other _____ _____

2. Share a skill. What skill do you have in which someone else has expressed an interest? Who expressed an interest?

❑ Business _____

❑ Gardening _____

❑ A hobby _____

❑ Cooking/baking _____

❑ Financial _____

❑ Home repair _____

❑ A sport _____

❑ Other _____ _____

3. Offer comfort or time. You have experienced life and have heard many life stories. You can listen and offer comfort. With whom can you be supportive in this way?

_____

4. Make a contribution. Share your time, energy and passion about what matters to YOU! What are you interested in?

_____

What Makes YOU Happy and Satisfied?

Leader's Guide

Submitted by Linda Prib, ADC

Purpose

To determine what factors in our lives play a role in finding happiness and meaning.

To see the positive side of life and nurture an 'attitude of gratitude.'

To determine what might be lacking in one's life.

Possible Names of Sessions

- "Flower Power"
- "Satisfaction Counts"
- "To Bloom and Grow"

Background Information

Past events along with life experiences, personal talents and cultural differences are only a few factors that influence how we define what makes us happy or satisfied with our lives. Analyzing one's life, in the here and now, is a valuable task.

Activity

1. Write on the board "What Makes YOU Happy and Satisfied"? Distribute handouts and explain that this session will focus on YOU as an individual.

2. Distribute handouts and easy-to-read pens or markers.

3. Ask group members to complete the flower by putting their first name in the line under SELF in the center of the flower.

4. Then, instruct group members to fill in the eight petals with whatever makes them happy or satisfied. Examples include: family, love, accomplishments, job, health, travel, freedom, job, owning a home, career or job, financial security, education, community. Emphasize there are no right or wrong answers and responses will vary. Explain that this is a reflection of today, not ten years ago or ten years in the future.

5. Share responses.

6. Process using any combination of comments/questions below or develop your own:
   a. Discuss the idea that we are all unique; our family and our life experiences have made us different. What has been a positive experience for you that influenced one of your answers?
   b. Discuss how we are like a flower, we bloom and develop in our own time and way. What type of flower are you? A slow-to-open rose, or a very quick-to-open daisy?
   c. Observe the flower drawing carefully. Each petal is a little different. It is not a perfect flower. Is anything in nature actually perfect? Each creation is unique and special. What is the most unique part of your flower? Explain.
   d. Do you look at others as being like that flower? Each one different and special? Tell us about someone you know that can be compared to a flower. Explain.
   e. Is there someone in your life that has helped you flower and grow? Who is this person, how did they effect you?
   f. Is there part of your flower that has not developed yet? Explain.
   g. How can you be a positive influence on someone else, so that they may grow?

Variations

1. Introduce group with the following icebreaker. Write four words on the board: health, money, fame, and love. Ask group members to choose only one word to answer the question: Which would make you the happiest and most satisfied? Discuss.

2. Create 'attitudes of gratitude' journals using the chosen petal themes for starters, "I am grateful that I have my _____. I feel satisfied because _____."

What Makes YOU Happy and Satisfied?

Who Am I Culturally?

Leader's Guide

Submitted by Elana Markowitz, OTRL

Purpose

To increase sense of self by identifying as a member of a cultural group.

To learn about the practices of other cultures.

Possible Names of Sessions

- "Pride In Who I Am!"
- "My Cultural Identity"
- "More Alike Than Different?"

Background Information

We live in a melting pot of different cultures. Unfortunately, however, many people are unfamiliar with the practices of people living around them. This lack of knowledge leads to stereotypes and prejudices. This activity is designed to give participants an opportunity to identify themselves as part of a cultural group, and teach others about the cultural practices of others. It might serve as an enlightening activity for any group where cultural differences are an issue.

Activity

1. Discuss the definition of a culture in general terms. What does a culture comprise of? What makes each culture unique? Do not allow members to share personal cultural experiences just yet.

2. Distribute handouts and easy-to-read pens.

3. Instruct group members to jot down a few words or draw images that represent their cultural backgrounds in each category.

4. Collect completed sheets and read aloud written responses.

5. Ask group members to guess which group member wrote each response.

6. Encourage group members to ask each other questions, but first discuss the appropriate ways to ask questions so as not to offend anyone.

Variations

1. Ask each group member/staff/family to bring in cultural foods and celebrate!

2. Lead group discussion on these topics:

   a. Where do stereotypes and prejudices come from?

   b. What role do each of us have today in perpetuating or preventing stereotypes and prejudice?

   c. How have we been affected by prejudice or stereotypes?

   d. What is a block that you could add to the handout? (E.g., art? country from which culture originally came from? dance? aromas?)

Who Am I Culturally?

My Culture	Language	Religion / Spiritual Practice

Food	Clothing	Music

Rituals	Holidays	Leader

What else is unique to your culture(s)?

A Year of Events and Traditions

Leader's Guide

Submitted by

K. Oscar Larson, OTL, MA, BCG

Purpose

To increase awareness of common interests during different times of the year.

Possible Names of Sessions

- "Enjoy the Season!"
- "What's So Special About This Time of Year?"
- "The Four Seasons"

Background Information

Seasons and holidays host different activities and celebrations. These days, whether preparing for them or engaging in them, give structure and continuity to our lives. People may prefer certain times of the year to other times, depending on their experiences and the activities available during those seasons and holidays. This activity allows group members to learn more about their common interests, develop awareness and trust of other group members, and see the difference between one day and another. This activity can be used for any time during the year, with emphasis on events around that time as well as throughout the year.

Activity

1. Distribute handouts and easy-to-read pens.

2. Ask group members to write three events for holidays and each season, focusing on what they enjoy.

3. Discuss the following questions:

   a. Who introduced these events and traditions into your life?

   b. Which did you develop on your own?

   c. Which bring the most meaning to you?

Variations

1. Write on the board: 1. Childhood; 2. Adolescence; 3. Adulthood. Ask group members to write three memorable events, one each from each period for each category (holiday and four seasons). Discuss.

2. Use this handout in conjunction with *Emotions Plus – A Lifetime of Feelings* – page 23. Ask group members to identify three emotions, which they associate with each season and for three holidays.

A Year of Events and Traditions

IDENTIFY SOME OF THE ACTIVITIES THAT YOU ENJOY DOING EACH YEAR

Spring

1. _____
2. _____
3. _____

Summer

1. _____
2. _____
3. _____

Fall

1. _____
2. _____
3. _____

Winter

1. _____
2. _____
3. _____

Holidays

1. _____
2. _____
3. _____

Acts of Loving Kindness

Leader's Guide

Purpose

To recognize how acts of loving kindness may add to the quality of life.

Possible Names of Sessions

- "Kindness Counts"
- "No Time Like the Present!"
- "It's Time To Share"

Background Information

It is beneficial to look at semi-retirement, retirement or a time of having fewer responsibilities, as a time to share. Sharing allows for a sense of connectedness with others and a desire to share a passion or enjoyment. Ideas to be shared are limitless and can be inspirational!

Activity

1. Begin with a discussion of what people remember about loved grandparents (or older neighbors or relatives). Focus especially on how they spent their time.

2. Distribute handouts with easy-to-read pens.

3. Explain concept of activity using left paragraph on handout and background information.

4. Read the following examples to your clients.
   a. Share my love of nature with <u>my granddaughter</u> by <u>taking her for walks in the park</u>.
   b. Share my love of nature with <u>my son-in-law</u> by <u>sharing my knowledge of bird-watching</u>.
   c. Share my love of nature with <u>my friend</u> by <u>taking him fishing</u>.

5. Give group members ten minutes to complete handout.

6. Encourage creativity and unique responses.

7. Share responses and problem solve ways that these ideas could actually happen. Discuss barriers to action and supports to facilitate action.

Variations

1. Create exciting groups or programs with participants by sharing any of the ideas that group members were enthusiastic about sharing! For example: "Bake a Bread with Marsha", "Listen to Violin by Harry", "Plant Seedlings with Luke".

2. Show a video clip of a favorite commercial, movie or TV show exemplifying an act of loving kindness from an older adult, e.g., *Cosby Show, Driving Miss Daisy, Judging Amy, Fried Green Tomatoes.*

Acts of Loving Kindness

We all have choices. We can choose to be giving and loving. OR…
We can choose to feel sorry for ourselves, be angry about our past and life's shortcomings. (Probably NOT a good choice!)

Performing acts of loving kindness is an approach towards healthful living. It is possible to be loving and giving despite obstacles we might face.

By giving of ourselves, we might also gain.

What might you gain if you choose to do acts of loving kindness?

_____

_____

Here are some ideas for how to get started.
Fill in the blanks if this idea is appealing to you:

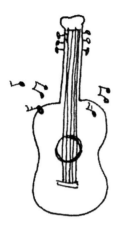

> SHARE MY LOVE OF NATURE WITH _____
>
> BY _____.

> SHARE MY LOVE OF MUSIC WITH _____
>
> BY _____.

> SHARE MY LOVE OF A HOBBY (_____)
>
> WITH _____
>
> BY _____.

> SHARE MY TIME WITH _____.

> VISITING WITH _____.

> SHARE MY LOVE OF COOKING (OR EATING!)
>
> WITH _____.

> YOUR OWN IDEA:
>
> SHARE MY _____
>
> WITH _____.

How To Make A Friend

Leader's Guide

Submitted by Linda Prib, ADC

Purpose

To explore the steps it takes to make friends.

Possible Names of Sessions

- "Never Too Old to Make a New Friend"
- "What Are Friends Good For, Anyways?"
- "Ya Gotta Have Friends"

Background Information

It has been proven that as we age we often have fewer opportunities for meeting new people and developing relationships. But friendships in older age can provide a tremendous source of satisfaction, support and interest to one's life. Friends can be a very positive force. Friends can have fun doing things together. They can share fond memories and be a valuable sounding board in a way that family sometimes cannot.

Activity

1. Distribute handouts and easy-to-read pens.

2. Discuss background information above and get group input as to meaning of friends, especially as one grows older.

3. Instruct group members to write the steps of making a friend, on the blank steps leading to the door.

4. Offer examples such as: enjoy each other's company, listen, bake a cake, write a letter, send a card, call on the telephone, say a kind word, smile.

5. Share completed handouts discussing similar and different responses. Discuss the challenges in making and keeping friends, as we get older.

6. Discuss any of these:

   a. What does it mean to be a 'good friend'?

   b. What do you like doing by yourself? What activities do you like to share with others?

   c. If you could have one friend to do something really special with you, what would you do together?

Variations

1. List mottos, expressions or sayings that have friendships or relationships in them: "Make new friends but keep the old, one is silver and the other's gold"; "A friend in need is a friend indeed"; "fair-weather friend"; "ships that pass in the night"; "The Golden Rule"; etc.

2. List places that people in the group could likely meet new friends.

How To Make A Friend

The road

to a friend's house

is never long.

The Social Skills Interview

Leader's Guide

Submitted by Kelly Fischer, OTR/L
and Kim Corbett, OTR/L

Purpose

To increase functional self-expression in the area of social skills.

Possible Names of Sessions

- "Here's.........."
- "HEADLINE: New Talk Show In Town"
- "Meet the Guest"

Background Information

Many people feel threatened or intimidated to share thoughts and feelings in a group setting. They may become quiet and withdrawn. This activity facilitates speaking in a group within a highly structured and supportive setting. Social skills is a great topic and how we relate to others is important when thinking of overall life satisfaction.

Activity

1. Briefly discuss the topic of social skills.
2. Explain to the group that they are going to be asked to discuss this topic by attending a new talk show in their city/town.
3. Distribute copies of the handout and easy-to-read pens.
4. Read aloud.
5. Each group member will be designated a role including: 1 host, 1 guest, audience members to ask questions (depending on group size) and remaining audience.
6. Designate these roles to each group member by one of three methods:
   a. Have group members choose roles independently
   b. Have group members choose slips of paper (roles as stated in 5. above) out of a basket or
   c. The group leader designates specific roles to certain group members
7. Explain the responsibilities of each talk show member as follows:
   a. Host - welcomes the audience, reads the script to the guest
   b. Guest - responds to the hosts questions
   c. Audience with questions - after all questions on the script are answered, these group members ask appropriate questions to the guest
   d. Remaining audience - listens to the interactions of host and guest, applauds when appropriate, critiques the host and guest on their social skills at the end of the talk show
8. Using the designated roles, act the talk show.
9. When complete, get feedback from audience on how well the host/guest played their roles.
10. Encourage group members to switch roles and continue to act the talk show until all have had a chance to be the host or guest or as long as time permits.

Variations

1. Make/bring props to create fun, talk show setting: microphone, desk, cue cards saying 'applause', etc.
2. Develop other game show scripts on topics of interest: leisure and fun, being a grandparent, money management skills.

The Social Skills Interview

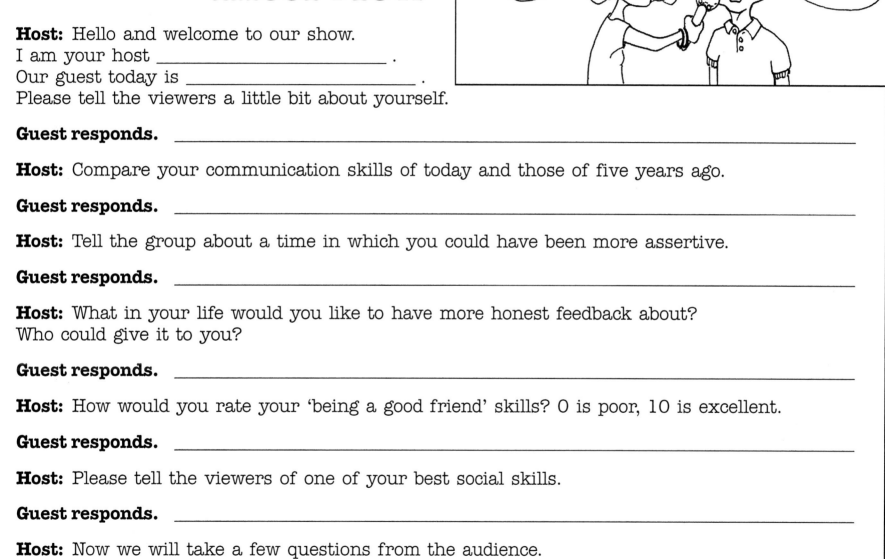

Host: Hello and welcome to our show.
I am your host _____ .
Our guest today is _____ .
Please tell the viewers a little bit about yourself.

Guest responds. _____

Host: Compare your communication skills of today and those of five years ago.

Guest responds. _____

Host: Tell the group about a time in which you could have been more assertive.

Guest responds. _____

Host: What in your life would you like to have more honest feedback about?
Who could give it to you?

Guest responds. _____

Host: How would you rate your 'being a good friend' skills? 0 is poor, 10 is excellent.

Guest responds. _____

Host: Please tell the viewers of one of your best social skills.

Guest responds. _____

Host: Now we will take a few questions from the audience.

WHAT I LIKE TO DO

Leader's Guide

Purpose

To increase leisure interests.

Possible Names of Sessions

- "Time Can be Well Spent"
- "Choices, Choices, Choices"
- "My Interest Level"

Background Information

There are many reasons older adults may want to rethink their leisure pursuits. People may be retired with more time than they are used to. Physical challenges might affect a person's ability to engage in leisure: poor eyesight, a stroke or shaky hands might influence leisure choices.

Typical leisure interest checklists often contain many activities an older adult doesn't do. This list, designed for seniors, may spark an old interest or create a new one.

Activity

1. Bring several possible leisure interests to group: a romance novel, a history book, a CD of music, needlepoint, kitchen bowl and spoon (to represent cooking), a hammer, word search puzzle book, a baseball, a plant (to represent gardening).

2. Ask group members, as you show each item, to say if this is of high interest, low interest or no interest.

3. Compare results.

4. Explain that leisure choices are individual and sometimes they change as we mature.

5. Distribute handouts and easy-to-read pens.

6. Give group members ten minutes to complete handout.

7. Discuss results.

8. Develop action plans based on responses and discussion.

Variations

1. If several members have similar interests, pair or group them together to make plans and support each other.

2. Create a second session with a local older adult enthusiast about a popular leisure topic. This person can demonstrate this skill and be a great role model!

WHAT I LIKE TO DO

name _____

Put an **H** for what you have a **High** level of interest in.
Put an **L** for what you have a **Low** level of interest in.
Put an **N** for what you have **No** interest in.

MUSIC
Listening to _____
Playing an instrument _____
Singing _____

ART
Doing craft projects _____
Appreciating art _____
Doing artwork as a
project with others _____

READING
Fiction books _____
Nonfiction books _____
Listening to
someone read _____
Poetry _____

SOCIAL
Conversation _____
Parties _____
Playing games / cards _____
Magazine / Newspaper _____

WRITING
Letters/Notes _____
Journal _____
Creative _____

SPORTS
Watching on TV _____
Going to events _____
Playing _____

BEING ACTIVE
Competitive sports _____
Stretching activities _____
Aerobic activities _____

FOOD RELATED
Baking _____
Cooking _____
Nutrition _____
Eating out! _____

HISTORY
World _____
Your country _____
Local _____
Military _____

MOVIES
Comedy _____
Action _____
Drama _____
Mystery _____

NATURE
Being outdoors _____
Looking outdoors _____
Appreciating nature
in videos or books _____

TV
Dramas _____
Sit-coms _____
Talk shows _____
News _____

COMPUTERS
Internet _____
Email _____
Online shopping _____

OTHER
_____ _____
_____ _____
_____ _____

What You DON'T Say Counts, Too!

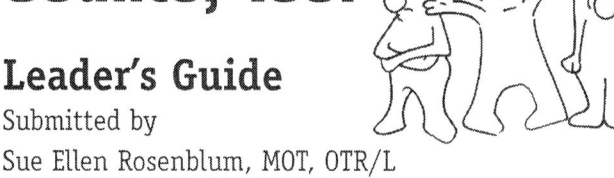

Leader's Guide

Submitted by
Sue Ellen Rosenblum, MOT, OTR/L

Purpose

To demonstrate the impact of nonverbal communication.

Possible Names of Sessions

• "Possible Miscommunications?"
• "What Am I Not Saying?"
• "Clear Communication...
  Giving the Benefit of the Doubt"

Background Information

It is easy and common to form opinions of others based on observations of their non-verbal communication including facial expression, body language, eye contact and posture. These perceptions may be inaccurate, incomplete and unfair. There are hundreds of instances daily where assumptions (and false assumptions) might be occurring involving family members, friends, neighbors, and even health care professionals! Recognizing this possibility and ways to combat this might be one way to increase positive social interactions and relationships.

Activity

1. Introduce the concept of nonverbal communication, either using people posing as examples or showing magazine clippings.

2. Distribute handouts and easy-to-read pens.

3. Ask group members to look at the three drawings on the handout and write their first assumption based on the person in the drawing.

4. Share responses.

5. Allow group members to provide other opinions about the people in the pictures.

6. Develop questions one might ask to validate or negate any possible assumptions. These questions should be able to answer: "How would we know if what we thought, was true?"

7. Now, ask group members to consider that they might be viewed as the pictures on the page. Someone like a roommate, friend, family member or healthcare professional might be assuming something they are doing has a meaning, and this meaning might be incorrect. How might they clear up communication?

Variations

1. Invite four people to "act" in a nonverbal way in the front of the room: 1. tired 2. angry 3. not wanting to be bothered 4. interested. Or use those nonverbal behaviors noticed that may be misconstrued by patients, residents or staff, e.g., falling asleep when someone is talking to them. Ask group members to write down impressions they get when they look at these people. Discuss perceptions and misperceptions.

2. Emphasize that trying to understand people from nonverbal communication and without conversation can be a disaster! The likelihood of misunderstanding is great. Ask creative group members to write a short (even funny) skit taken from real-life examples and to perform this in front of the group as a follow-up session.

What You DON'T Say Counts, Too!

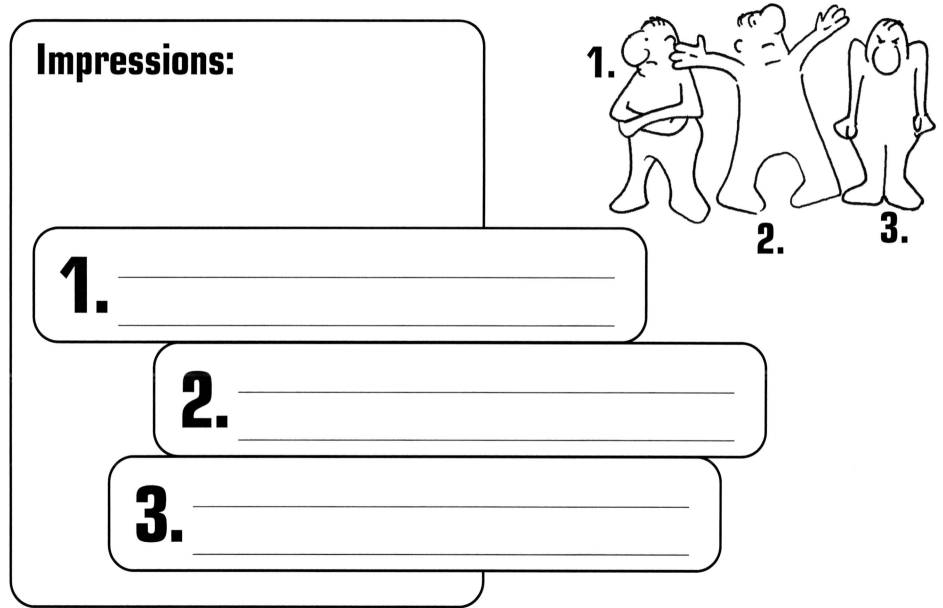

Impressions:

1. _____

2. _____

3. _____

My Love Letter to Me

Leader's Guide

Submitted by Rev. Donald Shields, BRE, MTS

Purpose

To nurture the spiritual side of our selves for developing or maintaining a healthy self-image.

Possible Names of Sessions

- "Loving Myself"
- "Seeking the Spiritual Side"
- "I Am Worth It!"

Background Information

It is rare to be able to create opportunities to talk about how we feel about ourselves in an open and supportive atmosphere. The nature of spirituality is that it attempts to connect us with the uniqueness that we are as human beings. Spiritual access to a healthy self-image might be a natural 'way in' for some older adults.

Activity

1. Discuss obstacles or barriers in developing or maintaining a healthy self-image.

2. Distribute handouts and pens, markers or colored pencils.

3. Read handout aloud and then give group members 10 minutes to complete.

4. Ask the following:

   a. Which was the easiest part to complete? The most difficult?

   b. In which of the three areas do you most want to explore or hear about how people responded?

5. Divide group into smaller groups to pursue discussing individuals' interests.

6. Reconvene and share what was interesting in the smaller groups.

Variations

1. Engage in brainstorming a list of how the facility or center can be more supportive in getting clients spiritual needs met. Take the list and share with people who could effectively make things happen.

2. Offer people an opportunity to be expressive and creative. Place markers, watercolors, colored pencils, etc., on table. Instruct people to use the back of their handout to complete the sentence: "Other spiritual pursuits that interest me right now are _____." Ask them to depict images or drawings rather than words. Play soft background music. Share in supportive atmosphere. Explore the role that art, music, and poetry might have in self-image or spirituality.

My Love Letter to Me

There are always positive and negative circumstances, events and people that influence how we perceive ourselves as to whether we are lovable or unlovable. Take some time to complete the following exercises.

I, _____,
resolve to love myself as a unique
individual in this world who has
worth, value, gifts to give and _____
_____
_____ .

One thing that I have going for me
is my _____
_____
_____ .

There is just one me – and I resolve
that one spiritual pursuit that I can
adopt right now is to embrace this
person called 'me'.

What people or actions allow me
to embrace myself as unique and
worthy of love? _____
_____
_____

What negative influences or attitudes
can you resolve to limit or overcome
their power in your life? _____
_____
_____
_____
_____
_____

THIS NEW YEAR'S RESOLUTION

Leader's Guide

Submitted by Rev. Donald Shields, BRE, MTS

Purpose

To create spiritual New Year's resolutions.

Possible Names of Sessions

- "Not Another Resolution!"
- "I Am Worthy of What?"
- "Why Wait for the New Year?"

Background Information

New Year's resolutions usually are about changing externals. This exercise helps group members see that their messages to themselves about themselves may need to be revised to include healthy spiritual truths about our uniqueness and worth.

You can use this activity ANY month, not just in late December, and call it "Why Wait for Next Year?"

Activity

1. Write the name of session on board and discuss why you chose that name.

2. Distribute handouts, easy-to-read pens and highlighters.

3. Instruct group members to highlight certain words or phrases on the handout that seem to have special meanings as the handout is read or completed.

4. Ask a group member to read first section. Instruct group members to fill in blanks and then share responses.

5. Read quote and ask group members to share thoughts.

6. Ask a group member to read section marked 'A RESOLUTION', filling in the blanks.

7. Give each group member an opportunity to stand, read his/her resolution and receive a sincere and hearty applause from the group. Resolutions might sound like: *In this next year, I will honor my spiritual needs by going to my place of worship two times a month; will make amends for wrongdoings and forgive myself; will tell people when I've done something I'm proud of; etc.*

Variations

1. Develop a large collage of "NEW New Year's Resolutions" in which everyone writes their resolutions on poster board with a thick marker.

2. Discuss what barriers there might be in people believing they are worthy of receiving the great things that life has to offer. Allow group members to support each other in recognizing their worthiness.

THIS NEW YEAR'S RESOLUTION

When we evaluate the different areas of our lives, and the impact those areas have, we often underestimate the value of our self-worth.

Hopefully – this year – you will be able to commit to allowing yourself the faith to believe you are worthy of…

- Love,
- Value,
- Good Things,
- Healthy Relationships,
- New Directions,
- _____,
- _____,
- and _____.

Just as we need faith to understand our place in the grand scheme of things, we also need to believe ourselves worthy of love, good and nurture.

"You yourself, as much as anybody in the entire universe, deserve your love and affection."

The Buddha

A RESOLUTION

Most of the time, people make New Year's Resolutions, and by February they are forgotten.

They revolve around diet, exercise, being nice or _____.

In the past, I have set New Year's Resolutions to

_____

_____

_____

_____

Develop a new type of New Year's Resolution – about learning to love and honor yourself:

In this next year, I _____

_____

_____

_____

Weathering Spiritual Seasons

Leader's Guide
Submitted by Rev. Donald Shields, BRE, MTS

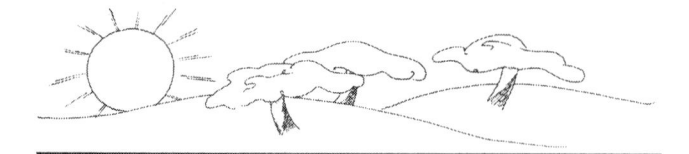

Purpose

To explore a variety of spiritual feelings and experiences.

Possible Names of Sessions

- "Let It Shine"
- "The Weather Outside Is Frightful, But..."
- "What Does It Take To Weather a Storm?"

Background Information

It is not unusual for persons recovering from a trauma or illness to buy into magical thinking wherein they pursue the "ideal" religious experience. This can lead to disappointment, discouragement, and perhaps abandoning of this important part of our lived experience. Exposing participants to a variety of "spiritual" 'seasons' may help normalize the highs and lows of those spiritual experiences.

Activity

1. Explain that our spiritual attitudes and lives are very much related to our healing selves.

2. Distribute handouts and easy-to-read pens.

3. Read left section together as a group and allow group members a few minutes to complete the lines.

4. Discuss and provide a supportive atmosphere for sharing. See if there are any similarities re: seasons or experiences.

5. Give time for group members to read and complete right section.

6. Divide group into triads.

7. Allow one group member to record all responses, one to monitor time and one to share with entire group.

8. Assign triad the task of discussing all of the sources of spiritual "light" listed in the second column and make a large list of all responses with no repeats. Give group ten minutes to complete.

9. Reconvene and share responses.

10. Discuss the possibilities available to bring the light into our lives.

Variations

1. Introduce concept of drawing a "seasonal vignette". This drawing should reflect how someone is feeling spiritually using a nature theme that will reflect the "artist's" spirit. Have available different art media.

2. Discuss how photographs can capture a sense of spirit. Collect photos and show to group one by one and ask them to reflect on how it moves and relates to them.

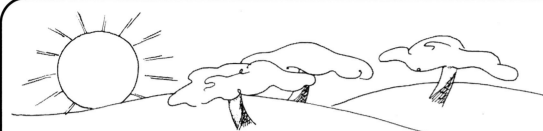

Weathering Spiritual Seasons

The spiritual patterns in our lives can be like weather patterns or seasons. There may be sunshine, sweltering heat, drought, hurricanes, fierce storms, refreshing rain, pelting hail and everything in between. Our personal experience and where we are in life may dictate our response to these varying conditions of the spirit.

In looking at the four seasons: winter, spring, summer, fall…is there one 'season' you are experiencing in your specific spiritual journey? Which one?

_____

What negatives would this season bring with it?

_____

(E.g., darkness, mud, blowing sand, burning heat)

What positives would this season bring with it?

_____

(E.g., rain, nurture, growth, beauty)

If we really think about it there are really no perfect seasons – just our response to them. And there are really no perfect states or places of being. With our humanity we bring personal experience.

What might be pleasing to one person may not be helpful for you. The spiritual quest or journey is not only identifying where our spirit is at, it's also adapting to the changing seasons.

Seasons and weather are dictated by the earth's relationship to its light source, the sun. Identifying our sources of spiritual "LIGHT" is important in understanding our own spiritual journey.

In the spaces below, list some sources of spiritual "light" that may be shining around you.

_____

_____

_____

_____

_____

EMPOWERING MYSELF TO BE ACTIVE!!!

Leader's Guide

Purpose

To recognize the barriers and benefits of being active in older age and to set action plans in motion.

Possible Names of Sessions

- "Use it or Lose It"
- "Active Lifestyles"
- "DO IT NOW!"

Background Information

For many people the notion of "exercise" connotes sweaty gyms, fanatics, athletes, hard work and sore muscles. A preferred context for some people might be "being active". This more inclusive term might be more appealing and less threatening and may yield activities that people can easily include in a more active lifestyle.

Activity

1. Describe typical complaints of people who don't lead an active lifestyle and list on the board. This list may include:
   - Tired
   - No energy
   - Irritable
   - Never get out of the house
   - Feel every ache and pain

2. Lead group in a five-minute walk (outside if possible).

3. Return and discuss how people feel. Hopefully responses will include more energy, more alive, etc.

4. Distribute handouts and easy-to-read pens.

5. Give group members ten minutes to complete entire handout EXCEPT 'action plan'.

6. Discuss openly possible barriers to being active in older age. Responses may include: fear of breaking a bone, lack of financial resources or no one to do activity with.

7. Support group members in addressing these issues safely and realistically allowing for group problem solving if appropriate.

8. Help group members design ACTION PLANS at bottom of page. Explain that the idea is to be committed to an idea and to gain forward motion.

9. Share as a group.

Variations

1. Depending on group setting, interests and action plans, make future plans with this group, e.g., once a week table tennis tournament, design an 'A.M. WALKING GROUP' for some or all participants, once a month BOWLING GROUP.

2. Bring possible motivators or conveniences to session and share:
   - Music
   - Light weights
   - Padded socks

EMPOWERING MYSELF TO BE ACTIVE!!!

Staying active, as an older adult can be very challenging. Peers may become less active, it may be hard to push yourself out the door in bad weather, and it may feel fruitless, BUT the consequences of being inactive may be damaging.

If I don't stay active, there is a greater chance that I....
(Write in your own in the blank spots)

will feel tightness of joints and muscles.

_____

will feel less energetic.

_____

will feel out of shape.

_____

will worry about my physical condition.

_____

will feel bored.

_____

won't be less interesting to be around.

_____

will not eat right.

_____

The rewards of staying active might be a life saver (or a quality-of-life saver). Here are a few helpful tips that might get you up and moving. Fill in the blanks with honest and realistic responses.

Do not overlook the simple things in life: walking and / or gardening. Both of these activities can have great benefits! Which one are you most likely to do?

❑ Walking　　　❑ Gardening

Other than walking and gardening activities, pick an activity you like. If you hate competitive sports, don't choose one! A hint to activity success is choosing what you like! What activity do you enjoy that you can do (even if it needs to be modified)?

_____

Do you like doing activities alone or with someone?

_____

If alone, what's an activity you can do alone?

_____

If with someone, who is someone you can contact that will participate with you? _____

_____

ACTION PLAN: _____

_____

_____

Energy Conservation

Leader's Guide

Submitted by Libby D. Schardt, OTR/L

Purpose

To increase knowledge of energy conservation, promoting safety in ADL's and home management.

To increase time for leisure or social pursuits, due to increased energy and decreased fatigue.

Possible Names of Sessions

- "Make Your Life Easier – Conserve Your Energy!"
- "Perfectionism Just Won't Work Now!"
- "I'll Save My Energy For _____"

Background Information

This activity might work well with those who are coming home after a hospitalization. Energy conservation relates overall to healing; it takes energy to heal and to recover. Obstacles to energy conservation may include: perfectionist attitude, lack of supports and being unaware of energy conservation techniques.

Activity

1. Introduce activity with background information.

2. Distribute handouts and easy-to-read pens.

3. Review the top portion of the handout, through GENERAL HINTS with group members. Use each point as a possibility for a discussion. Develop educational opportunities at any point, e.g., bring adaptive equipment to group and demonstrate: kitchen timer, raised toilet seat, wheeled cart.

4. Continue discussing the handouts using the blanks to share additional thoughts or ideas from the group.

5. After handout is completed, make a list on the board of what people want to conserve their energies for: playing with grandchildren, watching TV, reading, going out to eat, pursuing a hobby or interest, etc.

Variations

1. Use role plays as a way to practice offering and accepting help.

2. Develop index cards of situations that are potentially energy intensive: cleaning house, traveling, lawn work and gardening, getting ready for birthdays/holidays, doing laundry, getting dressed, buying gifts or any others that you feel group members might face. Have group members choose a card. Ask them to think of three possible ways to conserve energy with each situation.

Energy Conservation

means saving your energy for what you need it for the most!

You might be coming home after some type of an illness, procedure or episode that has been especially difficult or tiring. It might take your body and mind a while to recover. You don't want to expend your energy on things that don't really matter, and then, not have energy for what really matters.

HERE ARE SOME ENERGY CONSERVATION HELPFUL HINTS:

GENERAL HINTS

ALWAYS:

- Sit rather than stand
- Have objects (tools, equipment, utensils) close by and easy to reach
- Take more breaks rather than fewer breaks
- Use adaptive equipment if it is safer and easier
- Be willing to ask for help if you need
- Consider accepting offers for help
- Relax the "perfectionist" attitude
- _____
- _____

SPECIFIC HINTS

COOKING
- Use one-dish oven meals such as casseroles
- Plan meals ahead to ensure having all the ingredients
- _____

SHOPPING
- Check on grocery delivery services in your area and use if possible
- Have someone accompany you to the store to assist with the lifting and carrying
- _____

BATHING
- Sponge bathing can be an alternative to showers or tub baths
- Organize yourself with all the things that you need before you get started
- _____

I WANT MY INDEPENDENCE!

Leader's Guide

Purpose

To evaluate perceptions and actions which lend themselves to independence in older adults.

Possible Names of Sessions

- "I Want It MY Way!"
- "As Independent...As Possible!"
- "Realistic Aging...
  Looking at Independence Issues"

Background Information

A majority of older adults face the fear of losing control and independence. It might be a healthy approach to discuss fears in an open, nonjudgmental and realistic atmosphere. Recognizing personal fears and attitudes, and making personal choices about the environment, adaptive aids and services may encourage independence.

Activity

1. Write the word INDEPENDENCE largely on the board for all to see.

2. Ask group members what words or images come to mind when they see that word. List for all to see.

3. Explain that most people want to be as independent as possible and that there are attitudes and actions that might promote that.

4. Distribute handouts and pens.

5. First, focus on the statements on the left, allowing group members to share responses with the person on their left.

6. Proceed to the remaining statements on the right, and encourage sharing of actions that people do or don't do, in order to maintain independence, with the person on their right.

7. Ask each person to have one action plan, some action s/he can do which might promote independence. This might include discussing an attitude with a loved one, buying a piece of adaptive equipment, rearranging a shelf or pulling up a floor rug.

Variations

1. Bring a few adaptive equipment catalogues for people to peruse.

2. Find a poem, quote or saying about the value of independence and the value of accepting help as well.

I WANT MY INDEPENDENCE!

Independence means different things for different people. For some folks, it means living completely by themselves, for others, it means living with others and accepting help in certain areas, but doing things as independently as possible in other areas. And yet for others it's somewhere in the middle. Most of us like to feel like we are in control (or at least partial control!) and struggle with the balance between keeping ourselves as independent as possible and allowing others to help us.

Fear of becoming dependent can be overwhelming and create anxiety. As with most issues, it's better to talk about them rather than let them stay inside buried or hidden. Here are some thought provoking questions to address these concerns:

The challenges I face in aging are (financial, physical, emotional, etc.):

_____

_____.

I feel that accepting help means I'm a failure.

TRUE or **FALSE** (circle)

I feel that asking for help means I'm a failure.

TRUE or **FALSE** (circle)

I am pleasant to be around when I do need help.

TRUE or **FALSE** (circle)

(DISCUSS THESE REALITIES
WITH THE PERSON ON YOUR LEFT)

Now, read this checklist and honestly assess if you are helping yourself be as independent as possible.
Check what you do on a regular basis.

❏ I give myself extra time to be safe.

❏ I use adaptive equipment or aids that were recommended.

❏ I wear my glasses and/or hearing aid as needed.

❏ I walk with my walker or cane as recommended by my therapist/doctor.

❏ I take my medications as prescribed.

❏ I avoid clutter or things in the way that could create an unsafe environment.

❏ I spend money on things or services I need to help me be as independent as possible.

❏ I arrange my home or living area in a way that is safe, handy and easy-to-manage.

❏ I recognize that stairways and bathtubs are danger zones and I'm careful to take special precautions in those places.

❏ I accept help when needed.

(DISCUSS THE CHECKED STATEMENTS
WITH THE PERSON ON YOUR RIGHT)

Current Events!

Leader's Guide

Purpose

To engage cognitively about what is happening in the world with possible benefits of:

1. Reality orientation
2. Drawing attention away from an internal focus and moving towards an external focus
3. Interesting conversation and social interaction on relevant topics

Possible Names of Sessions

- "Keeping Up-To-Date"
- "The World Around Us"
- "Do You Know What's Happening?"

Background Information

There are a lot of reasons people lose touch with the outside world including disinterest, lack of stimulation or self-focus to the exclusion of others. Newspapers can be a perfect, non-threatening therapeutic media to use to re-enter the world! Talking about the news in a group setting can be a comfortable and shared experience. A structured, success-oriented session may pique an interest and provide a common ground for discussion.

Activity

1. Before session, read several articles in the local newspaper. Choose a variety of articles making sure there are more articles than the number of people in the group and that they are varied in interest and difficulty. Choose what might be of interest to your population and give choices of weather, movie reviews, sports, local politics, national news and an international story. Articles should be short enough to keep the person's attention and long enough to report on.

2. Explain group purpose in a language that group members understand and find meaningful.

3. Distribute handouts, highlighters and easy-to-read pens.

4. Give articles by interest and abilities.

5. Give group members ten minutes to prepare handouts.

6. Ask each group member to present the information written on the handout.

7. Facilitate conversations among group members as curiosity or interests are piqued.

Variations

1. Give favorite cartoons from the newspaper as a fun ending for the group.

2. Talk about what might be good topics for conversation starters in the next few days based on today's discussion.

Current Events!

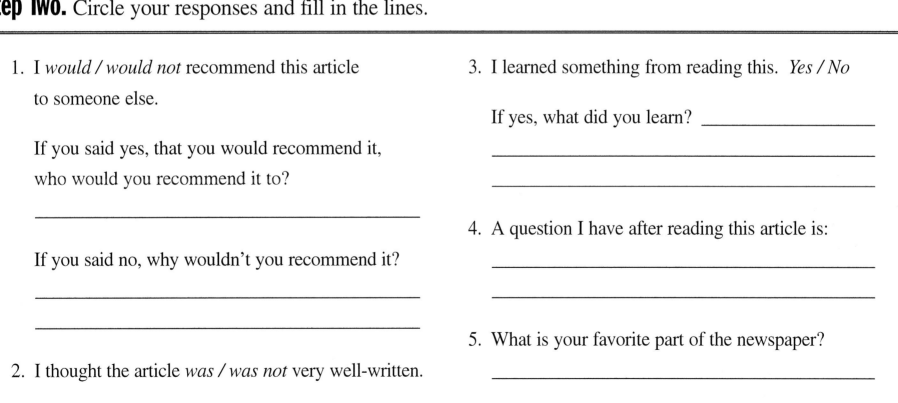

It's very important to know what's going on in the world and in your community.

Step One. Take your article and underline or highlight title and the main idea of the article. (One or two sentences)

Step Two. Circle your responses and fill in the lines.

1. I *would / would not* recommend this article to someone else.

   If you said yes, that you would recommend it, who would you recommend it to?

   _____

   If you said no, why wouldn't you recommend it?

   _____

   _____

2. I thought the article *was / was not* very well-written.

3. I learned something from reading this. *Yes / No*

   If yes, what did you learn? _____

   _____

   _____

4. A question I have after reading this article is:

   _____

   _____

5. What is your favorite part of the newspaper?

   _____

Mental Toughness – The Thinker Quiz

Leader's Guide

Submitted by
Libby D. Schardt, OTR/L

Purpose

To increase thought processing and group involvement by answering questions, listening, and sharing.

Possible Names of Sessions

- "It's So Hard to Think Sometimes!"
- "Brain Exercises"
- "Thought-full Questions"

Background Information

Answering challenging questions can be used as an entire activity or as a warm up activity to facilitate critical thinking and increase concentration to task. It also teaches the value of listening skills and attention to detail.

Activity

1. Distribute handouts and easy-to-read pens.

2. Give group ten minutes to individually complete handouts.

3. Divide group into smaller groups of 3-4 members. Give them time to discuss answers and decide on the "right" one.

4. Ask smaller groups to each share their best answer for each question.

5. Use ANSWER KEY to clarify if needed. Paper and pen might also be helpful in explaining challenging ones.

6. Give small token reward for team with most correct answers.

7. Ask group members for reasons this activity might be useful or helpful.

8. Engage in discussion of how to continue to challenge our minds.

Variations

1. Ask group members if they have any brainteasers to add to the list. Collect group members' contributions for future groups!

2. Distribute handouts and only give group members 5 minutes to complete as many as they can.

Answer Key

1. YES! All countries have a fourth of July...and a fifth, and a sixth, etc.

2. She is still alive.

3. ONE – the rest are just celebrations of the birth.

4. The match.

5. All of them!

6. 2.5 hours.

7. 1/2 way, he would then be running out.

8. 1 quarter and 1 nickel (it says that only one isn't a quarter).

9. Four.

10. They weren't playing each other.

11. 3 oranges.

12. If he were living, how would he have a widow?

Mental Toughness – The Thinker Quiz

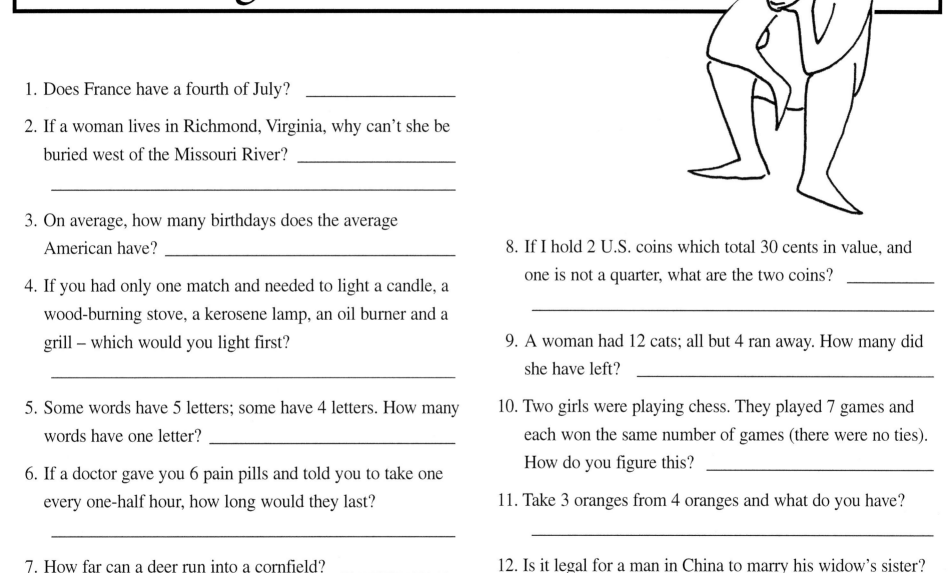

1. Does France have a fourth of July? _____

2. If a woman lives in Richmond, Virginia, why can't she be buried west of the Missouri River? _____

   _____

3. On average, how many birthdays does the average American have? _____

4. If you had only one match and needed to light a candle, a wood-burning stove, a kerosene lamp, an oil burner and a grill – which would you light first?

   _____

5. Some words have 5 letters; some have 4 letters. How many words have one letter? _____

6. If a doctor gave you 6 pain pills and told you to take one every one-half hour, how long would they last?

   _____

7. How far can a deer run into a cornfield? _____

   _____

8. If I hold 2 U.S. coins which total 30 cents in value, and one is not a quarter, what are the two coins? _____

   _____

9. A woman had 12 cats; all but 4 ran away. How many did she have left? _____

10. Two girls were playing chess. They played 7 games and each won the same number of games (there were no ties). How do you figure this? _____

11. Take 3 oranges from 4 oranges and what do you have?

    _____

12. Is it legal for a man in China to marry his widow's sister?

    _____

STRETCH
YOUR MIND

Leader's Guide

Purpose

To engage in creative, brain-boosting activities.

Possible Names of Sessions

- "Creative Thinking"
- "Thinking Outside the Box"
- "You Can Do It!"

Background Information

Creative brain boosting activities are success oriented, as they don't have right or wrong answers. They can be playful, interesting and offer a new view of an individual.

Activity

1. Distribute handouts and easy-to-read pens.

2. Emphasize that there are no right or wrong answers.

3. Instruct group members to do the first section. Offer an example on the flipchart if needed. Discuss responses. Support creativity and unique responses.

4. Instruct group members to do the second section. Offer an example on the flipchart if needed. Discuss responses. Support creativity and unique responses.

5. Instruct group members to answer the questions. Again, discuss the responses in an atmosphere of creativity.

Variations

1. Develop a list of creative questions or use these for more fun in a follow-up group or if time allows:

   a. If you were granted one wish that you could be sure would last for 100 years what would it be?

   b. If you could be responsible for one memorable 'first', what would it be? I'd be the first person to _____ .

   Collect one favorite response from each person, cut and paste to create a poster titled "OUR FAVORITES". Hang poster in a place where group members would like.

2. Find creative puzzle, optical illusion, and quiz books from a local bookstore or library and share.

STRETCH YOUR MIND

We can exercise our brain by doing or learning new and different things.
Creativity can stretch our minds. Here are three different types of exercise. Have FUN!

What could these drawings be? (There are no right or wrong answers.)

 1. _____

 2. _____

 3. _____

Finish the lines in any way that suits you.

 c.

 a.

 b.

I. What would you eat if you were granted one entire meal free of calories, fat or sugar?

_____
_____
_____

II. If you could invent a machine that would make your day easier or more pleasant, what would it do? ___

_____
_____
_____

III. What would you call it? _____

_____
_____

The "AND" Game

Leader's Guide

Purpose

To serve as a brain boosting activity.

Possible Names of Sessions

- "Think Again!"
- "AND So On!"
- "Come On...You Can Do It!"

Background Information

Cognitive activities can be success-oriented, stimulating and fun. The prompts that come before the 'and' are from a variety of sources including TV, books, songs, poems, food, childhood games, and idioms.

Activity

1. Introduce concept of using the brain like a muscle. It needs exercising and the way to do it is challenging it.

2. Distribute handouts and easy-to-read pens. Instruct group members to write best answer down. Even though there are many answers that MIGHT be right, there is one preferred answer.

3. Give group members as long as it takes to complete the handout. Use the key at right to check for answers.

4. Share responses.

5. Process the value of challenging the mind in fun and enjoyable ways.

Variations

1. Use as a timed activity giving a fun prize to the winner for an entire activity or as an icebreaker.

2. Play in pairs, with one person giving the clues and one receiving. Allow one hint if the guesser doesn't get it right on the first try.

Key

Jack and **Jill**

Washer and **dryer**

War and **Peace**

George and **Gracie**

Abercrombie and **Fitch**

The Birds and the **Bees**

Batman and **Robin**

Earth, Wind and **Fire**

Spencer Tracy and **Katherine Hepburn**

Cops and **Robbers**

Harpo, Groucho, Zeppo and **Chico**

Dagwood and **Blondie**

Sodom and **Gemorrah**

Rock, paper and **scissors**

Kiss and **Tell**

Beauty and the **Beast**

Salt and **Pepper**

Red, white and **blue**

Up, up and **away**

Lone Ranger and **Tonto**

Cheese and **crackers**

Porgy and **Bess**

Peanut butter and **jelly**

Amos and **Andy**

Fibber McGee and **Molly**

The Good, Bad and the **Ugly**

Bonnie and **Clyde**

Sears and **Roebuck**

Reading, Writing and **'Rithmetic**

In and **out**

Peter, Paul and **Mary**

Peter and the **Wolf**

Bagels and **cream cheese**

Liver and **onions**

Fred and **Wilma**

Macaroni and **cheese**

Bert and **Ernie**

Hot and **Cold**

The "AND" Game

Try these Brain Boosters for fun!
Fill in the blanks with the best possible answer.

Jack and _____

Washer and _____

War and _____

George and _____

Abercrombie and _____

The Birds and the _____

Batman and _____

Earth, Wind and _____

Spencer Tracy and _____

Cops and _____

Pots and _____

Harpo, Groucho, Zeppo and _____

Dagwood and _____

Sodom and _____

Rock, paper and _____

Kiss and _____

Beauty and the _____

Salt and _____

Red, white and _____

Up, up and _____

Lone Ranger and _____

Cheese and _____

Porgy and _____

Peanut butter and _____

Amos and _____

Fibber McGee and _____

The Good, Bad and the _____

Bonnie and _____

Sears and _____

Reading, Writing and _____

In and _____

Peter, Paul and _____

Peter and the _____

Bagels and _____

Liver and _____

Fred and _____

Macaroni and _____

Bert and _____

Hot and _____

The "AND" Game Challenge Edition

Leader's Guide

Purpose

To serve as a brain boosting activity.

Possible Names of Sessions

- "Think Again!"
- "Wanna Feel Challenged?"
- "Come On...You Can Do It!"

Background Information

Cognitive activities can be success-oriented, stimulating and fun. The prompts that come before the 'and' are from a variety of sources including TV, books, songs, poems, food, childhood games, and idioms. This challenge edition is for quick-minded people or those who were very successful at *The And Game* (page 72).

Activity

1. Introduce concept of using the brain like a muscle. It needs exercising and the way to do it is challenging it.
2. Distribute handouts and easy-to-read pens. Instruct group members to write best answer down. Even though there are many answers that MIGHT be right, there is one preferred answer. Give group members as long as it takes to complete the handout. Use the key on the right to check for answers.
3. Share responses.
4. Ask group to think of new *Now It's Your Turn* AND words and to challenge each other.
5. Process the value of challenging the mind in fun and enjoyable ways.

Variations

1. Use as a timed activity giving a fun prize to the winner for an entire activity or as an icebreaker.
2. Play in pairs, with one person giving the clues and one receiving. Allow one hint if the guesser doesn't get it right on the first try.

Key

The Pit and the **Pendulum**
Fric and **Frac**
Bell, Book and **Candle**
Horse and **buggy**
Martin and **Lewis**
Love and **marriage**
Frankie and **Johnnie**
Hook, line and **sinker**
Larry, Curly and **Moe**
Oil and **vinegar**
Tippecanoe and **Tyler Too**
Parsley, **Sage**, **Rosemary** and **Thyme**
The Good, the Bad and the **Ugly**
Mutt and **Jeff**
Samson and **Delilah**
Borrowed and **blue**
Baltimore and **Ohio**
Rogers and **Hammerstein**
Burns and **Allen**
Atcheson, **Topeka** and the **Santa Fe**
Raining cats and **dogs**
Bogie and **Bacall**

Lewis and **Clark**
Gilbert and **Sullivan**
PB and **J**
Tortoise and the **Hare**
Stars and **Stripes**
Tooth and **nail**
Cream and **sugar**
Footloose and **fancy free**
Fast and **furious**
Rough and **ready**
Ketchup and **mustard**
Rock and **Roll**
Birds and **bees**
Snap, **Crackle** and **Pop**
Up, up and **wway**
Hepburn and **Tracy**
Hook and **ladder**
Snow White and the **Seven Dwarves**
Assault and **battery**
Pat and **Mike**
Comedy and **tragedy**
Slow and **steady**
Savings and **Loan**
Field and **Stream**
Cat and **dog**
Starsky and **Hutch**
Peter, Paul and **Mary**

The "AND" Game - Challenge Edition

The Pit and the _____

Fric and _____

Bell, Book and _____

Horse and _____

Martin and _____

Love and _____

Frankie and _____

Hook, line and _____

Larry, Curly and _____

Oil and _____

Tippecanoe and _____ _____

Parsley, _____, _____
    and _____

The Good, the Bad and the _____

Mutt and _____

Samson and _____

Borrowed and _____

Baltimore and _____

Rogers and _____

Burns and _____

Atcheson, _____
   and the _____ _____

Raining cats and _____

Bogie and _____

Lewis and _____

Gilbert and _____

PB and _____

Tortoise and the _____

Stars and _____

Tooth and _____

Cream and _____

Footloose and _____ _____

Fast and _____

Rough and _____

Ketchup and _____

Rock and _____

Birds and _____

Snap, _____ and _____

Up, Up and _____

Hepburn and _____

Hook and _____

Snow White and the _____ _____

Assault and _____

Pat and _____

Comedy and _____

Slow and _____

Savings and _____

Field and _____

Cat and _____

Starsky and _____

Peter, Paul and _____

NOW IT'S YOUR TURN:

_____ and _____

_____ and _____

_____ and _____

_____ and _____

_____ and _____

Which / Witch Is It?
Leader's Guide

Purpose

To use words (homonyms) as a brain boosting activity.

Possible Names of Sessions

- "Use It or Lose It"
- "Sound-Alikes"
- "Boost Your Brain Sells"

Background Information

We read and hear homonyms all day, but many go unnoticed until we actually need to think of them. Thinking of them can be a very fun and challenging activity.

Activity

1. Introduce topic by giving homonym examples: road and rode, peace and piece, knows and nose.

2. Distribute handouts and easy-to-read pens.

3. Give group fifteen to twenty minutes to complete.

4. Score to see winner and give token prize.

5. Celebrate everyone's thinking powers!

Variations

1. Offer this as a timed exercise for added competitive spirit. First player with 30 points wins!

2. Use as a team game, everyone in the team gets a handout to look at, but only one recorder writes answers for group. Give all groups a pre-determined amount of time to complete the handout. Team with the most points wins!

Key

Sea / **see**	Lo / **low**
Witch / **which**	Hole / **whole**
There / **their**	Blue / **blew**
Sew / **so**	Red / **read**
Pane / **pain**	I / **eye**
Ate / **eight**	Wear / **ware**
Bore / **boar**	Pi / **pie**
Knight- **night**	Bow / **bough**
Know / **no**	Grown / **groan**
Be / **bee**	Toe / **tow**
Ant / **aunt**	Beach / **beech**
Threw / **through**	Sell / **cell**
Hair / **hare**	Mite / **might**
Hi / **high**	Soul / **sole**
Loan / **lone**	Sale / **sail**
Byte / **bite**	Grate / **great**
Bare / **bear**	Die / **dye**
Dear / **deer**	Foul / **fowl**
Here / **hear**	Tee / **tea**
	Flea / **flee**

Which /Witch Is It ?

HOMONYMS are words that sound the same but are spelled differently. Fill in the blanks.

SCORING: 1 point for each blank.

Sea / _____

Witch / _____

There / _____

Sew / _____

Pane / _____

Ate / _____

Bore / _____

Knight / _____

Know / _____

Be / _____

Ant / _____

Threw / _____

Hair / _____

Hi / _____

Loan / _____

Byte / _____

Bare / _____

Dear / _____

Here / _____

Lo / _____

Hole / _____

Blue / _____

Red / _____

I / _____

Wear / _____

Pi / _____

Bow / _____

Grown / _____

Toe / _____

Beach / _____

Sell / _____

Mite / _____

Soul / _____

Sale / _____

Grate / _____

Die / _____

Foul / _____

Tee / _____

Flea / _____

TOTAL POINTS : _____

Which /Witch Is It –
The Challenge Edition

Leader's Guide

Purpose

To use words (homonyms) as a brain-boosting activity.

Possible Names of Sessions

- "Challenge Yourself – REALLY!"
- "Sound-Alikes 2"
- "Boost Your Brain Sells – The Challenge Edition"

Background Information

We read and hear homonyms all day, but many go unnoticed until we actually need to think of them. Thinking of them can be a very fun and challenging activity.

Activity

1. Introduce topic by giving homonym examples: road and rode, peace and piece, knows and nose.

2. Distribute handouts and easy-to-read pens.

3. Give group fifteen to twenty minutes to complete.

4. Ask players if anyone had any *Find Your Own* answers and share.

5. Score to see winner and give token prize.

6. Celebrate everyone's thinking powers!

Variations

1. Give favorite cartoons / crossword puzzles from the newspaper as a fun ending for the group.

2. Talk about what might be good topics for conversation starters in the next few days based on today's discussion.

Key

Clause / **claws**

Horse / **hoarse**

Taught / **taut**

Doe / **dough**

Lie / **lye**

Clothes / **close**

Wry / **rye**

Lean / **lien**

Time / **thyme**

Pale / **pail**

Paws / **pause**

Bell / **belle**

Ball / **bawl**

Need / **knead**

TRI-NYMS

By / **buy** / **bye**

Fore / **four** / **for**

Too / **to** / **two**

Pare / **pear** / **pair**

Due / **do** / **dew**

Right / **write** / **rite**

So / **sew** / **sow**

Which / Witch Is It – The Challenge Edition

Welcome to the Challenge edition of this fun, word game!

HOMONYMS are words that sound the same but are spelled differently.

Fill in the blanks.

SCORING:

1 point for each blank.

FIND YOUR OWN are worth double and are 2 points per blank.

HOMONYMS

Clause / _____

Horse / _____

Taught / _____

Doe / _____

Lie / _____

Clothes / _____

Wry / _____

Lean / _____

Time / _____

Pale / _____

Paws / _____

Bell / _____

Ball / _____

Need / _____

TRI-NYMS

By / _____ /

_____

Fore / _____ /

_____

Too / _____ /

_____

Pare / _____ /

_____

Due / _____ /

_____

Right / _____ /

_____

So / _____ /

FIND YOUR OWN

_____ /

_____

_____ /

_____

_____ /

_____

_____ /

_____

_____ /

_____

TOTAL POINTS :

_____

❏ **Adults**　❏ **Older Adults**　❏ **Teens**

(Check one or more of the above for your intended audience.)

SUBMISSION ENTRY FORM

Save this form and submit one per handout. Photocopy if submitting more than one. Please print clearly – Thanks!

Name: _____

Profession: _____

Professional initials / credentials (if applicable): _____

Home street address: _____ Suite/Apt.: _____

City: _____ State: _____ Zip: _____

Phone: _____ Fax: _____

Home e-mail: _____ (write clearly, please)

Place of employment: _____ Dept.: _____

Street address: _____ Suite/Apt.: _____

City: _____ State: _____ Zip: _____

Phone: _____ Fax: _____

OK to fax you at work? _____ E-mail: _____
(write clearly, please)

Comments about handout (anything you want us to know or consider):

_____

_____

_____

_____

Name of handout:

_____

Topic: _____

❏ Original handout
❏ Original graphics
❏ Idea or sketch of graphics

Your signature confirming that this entry submission is your original work and that Wellness Reproductions and Publishing, LLC., has your permission to publish submitted handout with appropriate adaptations.

_____
Signature

_____
Date

If this submission is accepted for inclusion in a reproducible activity handout book. Wellness Reproductions and Publishing will create your handout and facilitator's guide and ask for your written approval as well as a one paragraph bio. $100 will be compensated for each accepted handout and each person whose handout(s) is published will receive a complimentary book.

Mail to:
WELLNESS REPRODUCTIONS & PUBLISHING
P.O. Box 9120
Plainview, NY 11803-9020